FLY FISHING FOR T

Bob Church and Peter Gathercole WITHDRAWN

2007

Fly Fishing for Trout

Bob Church and Peter Gathercole

The Crowood Press

First published in 1995 by
The Crowood Press Ltd
Ramsbury, Marlborough
Wiltshire SN8 2HR

www.crowood.com

Paperback edition 1998

This impression 2004

British Library Cataloguing-in-Publication Data
A catalogue record for this book is available from the British Library.

ISBN 1 86126 155 1

All photographs by Peter Gathercole

Line drawings by Christine Hart-Davies

Photograph previous page: well beaten, and ready to be slid over the
submerged net; a classic display of how it is done

Typeset and designed by D&N Publishing, Lambourn Woodlands,
Berkshire

Phototypeset by FIDO Imagesetting, Witney, Oxfordshire

Printed and bound in Malaysia by Times Offset (M) Sdn Bhd

CONTENTS

INTRODUCTION

Fly-fishing for trout has genuine international appeal. From the USA and Canada, across to Scandinavia, down through much of the rest of Europe, and south to Australia and New Zealand, Argentina and Chile, brown and rainbow trout provide a challenge found in no other freshwater fish. That they readily take an artificial fly, fight extremely hard, and are to be found in a wide range of temperate habitats accounts for much of this appeal. It is something in which man has played a large part, extending the trout's distribution, particularly in the Southern Hemisphere, and making it a truly global sport-fish. We have fished the fly for trout in most of these countries, and we hope that many more who are adventurous of spirit will join us in the future.

But with the popularity of fly-fishing continuing to grow, the need remains for comprehensive instruction for beginners and improvers, and even for more experienced anglers who may not be *au fait* with a particular technique. Many books which purport to be instructional fail in a number of areas, either through basic omissions or misinformation, or through inexperience on the part of the author; others because they offer the reader large tracts of indigestible copy from which the relevant information can be extracted only with difficulty.

Our intention in this book is to provide a new approach to fly-fishing instruction. Through the extensive use of location photography, the major techniques used for fishing both trout and grayling have been given a clarity and ease of understanding in keeping with the modern, highly visual approach used in many popular specialist titles.

Both stillwater and river fisheries are covered, from man-made reservoirs to large, natural lakes, from chalkstreams to rough rain-fed rivers. Each group is tackled by concentrating on the changing seasons and the changing techniques used to cope with prevailing conditions and insect hatches. And each chapter is brought to life by taking the reader through a particular set of circumstances which typify the technique being discussed.

Much of the pleasure of fly-fishing for trout comes from solving the ever-changing problems posed by new conditions and hatches: the authors take the reader to the waterside with them, bringing the task of instruction to its logical and most effective conclusion.

1 IMITATING THE TROUT'S NATURAL FOOD

The link between the natural insect and the artificial is intrinsic to the philosophy of fly-fishing. More practically, it provides an important key when deciding just what fly to attach to the end of the line. Indeed, a large proportion of the patterns we use are either a direct representation of a specific creature or give an impression of being something alive and edible.

Trout have catholic tastes and eat any creatures small enough to be swallowed. These can range from minute reed-smuts and animal plankton, such as daphnia, to something as large as another fish. It all depends on what is available at the time. However, when a specific food-form prevails, trout can become tuned-in to the extent that they will ignore all other forms along with any fly pattern which doesn't look or behave like the creature they are eating. This specialized feeding pattern is known as preoccupation, a phenomenon which occurs on most if not all waters.

If you have heard of preoccupation and believe it to concern only selectively feeding trout in clear chalkstreams, then think again. Stillwater trout can be just as selective and demand exactly the same reasoned approach if they are to be fooled consistently. Even if a trout isn't truly preoccupied, mimicking the form and movement of its most abundant prey is usually a much more effective technique than trying a general pattern. And this doesn't relate only to small flies. 'Fry-bashing' trout in a big lake can be just as selective in their feeding as those sipping down spent sherry spinners on the Itchen. If they are hitting shoals of 3in-long roach or are taking dying perch fry off the surface, then that is what you have to imitate.

The point of this example is to illustrate that imitating the trout's food *is* important. True, a great many fish are caught on general patterns, but when fish are feeding selectively, you don't have to be the one to watch a marvellous opportunity pass by. The ability to recognize what the fish are taking is a basic skill of fly-fishing, and the ability to identify the type of creature, its size, colour and habits go a long way to improving

any angler's knowledge and understanding of this fascinating pastime.

Studying all the creatures which the trout eat can be an absorbing subject in itself. However, the fly-fisher needs only a basic grasp. It is not necessary to be able to identify every species you see; in fact, many insects are all but impossible to identify as species out in the field. What is useful, though, is to know what the various types look like; for instance, the difference between a caddis and a mayfly or how a damselfly nymph appears in the water. Imitations are based on the size, shape and colour of the creature being copied, and as long as we understand that, we are well on the way to fishing imitatively.

Exactly what trout do eat can be broken down into four main groups. First are the aquatic insects, invertebrates which spend at least part of their lives beneath the water, usually in their immature stages. Included here are the Orders Ephemeroptera, or upwinged flies; Tricoptera, often called caddis-flies or sedges; Plecoptera or stoneflies; Odonata, which includes the dragonflies and damselflies; and Diptera, which includes the chironomid midges and reed-smuts, *Simulium* species.

The second group includes crustacea and bugs such as shrimps, hog-lice, snails, leeches and corixae, while the third covers all the small bait-fish such as perch, roach, bream and bullheads.

The fourth, the terrestrials, encompasses all those land-borne creatures which inadvertently fall into the water on occasion. They range from flies, beetles, grasshoppers and spiders right up to small mammals such as mice and voles!

EPHEMEROPTERA

The name 'ephemeroptera' describes the ephemeral nature of this group of insects. In reality only the winged adult ephemerids are short-lived; the nymphs of some species live for a year or more. This group

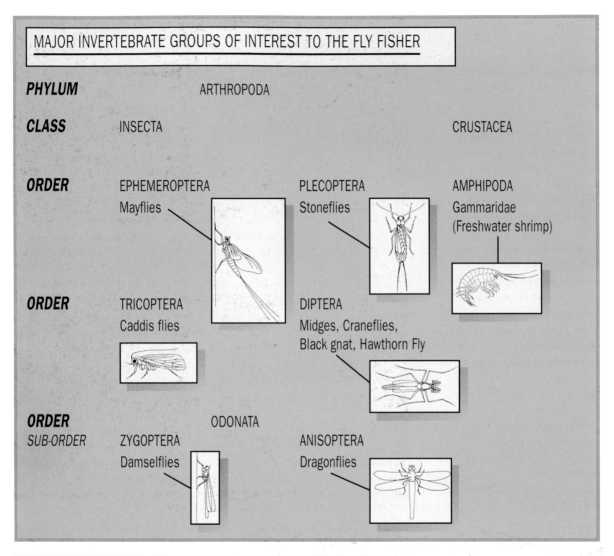

MAJOR INVERTEBRATE GROUPS OF INTEREST TO THE FLY FISHER

PHYLUM ARTHROPODA

CLASS INSECTA   CRUSTACEA

ORDER EPHEMEROPTERA   PLECOPTERA   AMPHIPODA
Mayflies   Stoneflies   Gammaridae
(Freshwater shrimp)

ORDER TRICOPTERA   DIPTERA
Caddis flies   Midges, Craneflies,
Black gnat, Hawthorn Fly

ORDER ODONATA
SUB-ORDER ZYGOPTERA   ANISOPTERA
Damselflies   Dragonflies

Members of the genus *Ephemera* are the largest of our upwinged flies. Their main emergence period is from the last weeks of May through to mid-June, and for this reason they have been given the name mayfly. This particular specimen is a male dun of the species *Ephemera vulgata*. It has just hatched and is clinging to a grass stem before transposing into the imago or spinner.

includes all the upwinged flies, or olives, plus the mayfly; insects which form the base of imitative fly-fishing, particularly on rivers.

They vary in size from the diminutive *Caenis*, at only one-eighth of an inch, right up to the mayfly *Ephemera danica*, the females of which may have a body-length of more than 1in. All have basically the same profile: a slim, slightly tapering abdomen tipped with two or three long tails, six legs, and a pair of large wings held upright and together when at rest. The wings give the flies the appearance of small sail-boats as they drift off downwind or downstream. Most species in fact have two pairs of wings, but the second is small and often difficult to see. In some species these hind wings are nothing more than a spur, and in a few, such as *Caenis* and *Cloeon* species, they are absent.

Ephemeroptera have three major stages in their life-cycle. After the egg, the immature aquatic stage is the nymph. This is usually camouflaged olive and brown to avoid detection by predators and

Nymphs of the mayflies (*Ephemera*) are large and pale-bodied, living for most of the time concealed within silt burrows. When fully developed, and about ¾in long, they rise through the water column towards the surface. However, their coloration makes them obvious and easy targets for predators such as trout.

Ephemera Nymph. The nymphs of the various species of the genus *Ephemera* are large, pale creatures adapted to burrowing in silt. This pattern uses ostrich herl to mimic the pulsating gills which run along the sides of the insect's abdomen and provide a seductive halo effect.

Flexibody Nymph. This pattern is designed to mimic a wide range of Ephemerid species. The Flexibody strip, which is used for the body, produces a delicate segmented effect which is ideal for imitating the body of the species ranging from the lake olive to many other Baetid species such as the large dark olive, pale watery or iron blue. All you have to do is alter the size and body shade to match the natural.

10

Nymphs of the family Baetidae exhibit the typical olive-nymph profile, with a slim, slightly tapering abdomen, a row of gills on either side, an enlarged thorax and three tails. It is the shape to use when imitating the nymphs of most river and stillwater upwinged species. These nymphs occur in a wide range of shades, depending on the species, from a light yellowish-olive through to dark olive or almost black.

is often marvellously adapted to suit its environment. Some nymphs, such as those of the March brown, *Rhithrogena germanica*, are dorsally flattened, the body and gills providing suction, helping them to grip on to stones and preventing them being pulled off by the swift current in which they live.

The nymphs of other, more sedentary species, such as of the blue-winged olive, *Ephemerella ignita*, crawl through moss and weed-fronds. Those of the *Baetids*, however, which include many river species such as the iron blue and the large dark olive, along with two major lake species, the pond and lake olives, are quick and able swimmers, and often referred to as 'agile darters'. The size of the imitation depends on the individual

The lake olive, *Cloeon simile*, is a major species on waters ranging from the great loughs and lochs of Ireland and Scotland through to the rich lowland reservoirs of southern England. Its main hatches occur during May and June, though a second generation appears in late summer/early September. Look for hatches taking place from late morning into the afternoon. This individual is a female sub-imago, or dun. It can be identified in the field by its two tails and the absence of hindwings.

Hatches of our largest mayfly, *Ephemera danica*, are a common sight on many rivers, particularly the chalk-streams of southern England, during the last week of May and into early June. The females are usually larger and more brightly coloured than the males and may be more than 1in long. Hatches are prolific, and at first the fish take imitations of the natural with little caution. However, they soon become selective and only a well-designed imitation will catch them.

Wonderbody mayfly. When imitating large insects, such as *Ephemera danica*, it is important that the pattern is light and the body soft. If the body is too stiff many of the more cautious fish will simply bump the fly without taking it properly. The Wonderbody mayfly uses a single white cock hackle to form a detached body that simply collapses as the fish takes, providing minimum resistance.

species. Imitations of the smaller *Baetids* need to be tied on hooks as small as size 20, though for larger species, such as those of the large dark olive, *Beatis rhodani*, or the lake olive *Cloeon simile*, a size 14 is about right. Patterns such as the simple Olive Nymph or the Flashback Olive are two effective tyings.

The other major group is formed by the burrowers; these are the nymphs of the mayflies, including *Ephemera danica* and *E. vulgata*. They are large, pale-bodied nymphs, and the fact that they spend their lives concealed within a burrow means that this coloration doesn't give them away to predators until it is time to

A species usually found on rivers, though it does occur on some lakes, is the blue-winged olive *Ephemerella ignita*. It is one of the major species for the river fly-fisher, and is probably the most widespread of all our upwinged species. The BWO is readily identified by its large smoky-blue wings and three tails. This specimen is a female dun. Look for hatches from mid-June right through to October, usually starting in early afternoon.

BELOW Lake Olive (left) and Blue Winged Olive (right) CDC Duns. The oily feather (cul-de-canard) found around the preen gland of various duck species makes a superb winging material for imitations of upwinged fly duns. Using the basic thorax-hackle tie with the hackle clipped under the shank, hook size, body colour and wing shade may be altered to mimic various species.

transpose. Richard Walker's original mayfly Nymph is still a deadly imitation, proving equally effective on both rivers and stillwaters.

Once the nymph has reached maturity, it rises to the surface and transforms into the next stage, the dun or sub-imago. This occurs either when the nymph has crawled out onto a stone or at the water's surface, the latter event making the emerging insect particularly vulnerable. The dun is usually matt, the wings often grey or coloured, the body dull olive or brown, though a few species, such as the yellow May dun, are bright yellow. Although winged, this sub-imago is still not sexually mature and soon after emerging from its nymphal skin it flies off to find cover in bankside vegetation. Patterns such as the CDC Dun, a simple Olive F Fly or a Poly-wing Dun can be tied in various sizes, colours and

BELOW A few minutes, or hours, after the dun has emerged, it transposes into the imago, or spinner. Concealed behind a leaf or stem, the spinner works itself free of the skin of the more sombre-hued dun, even shedding a layer of skin from its already delicate wings. This is a female lake olive, *Cloeon simile*.

RIGHT Once the dun has transposed into the sexually mature imago, or spinner, it is ready to reproduce. This male lake olive spinner sits patiently behind a blade of grass, waiting to join the mating swarms.

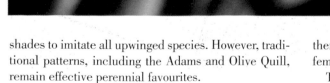

shades to imitate all upwinged species. However, traditional patterns, including the Adams and Olive Quill, remain effective perennial favourites.

After a few minutes or hours, depending on temperature and species, the skin along the back of the dun's thorax splits and the imago, or spinner, works itself free. This is a much brighter creature, the wings often clear, the body bright and sparkling. Now the insect is ready to reproduce. On a still summer's evening, it is common to see great swarms of male spinners dancing in mid-air, waiting for the females to join them and then to mate. The males' job is then over, but the females must return to the water to lay their eggs.

This is achieved in different ways by different species. Some dip their abdomen repeatedly into the water, releasing a few eggs at a time; others release all their eggs at one go in a ball or package. Yet others, including a number of the family *Baetidae*, crawl beneath the water's surface and deposit their eggs on a convenient stone or piece of weed. But all have one thing in common: no matter which species, once the female's task is complete, she dies.

The female spinner of the mayfly, *E. danica.* From the creamy-yellow of the dun emerges the spinner, a sparkling creature with clear wings veined heavily with black and a contrasting ivory-coloured body which looks pure white in the air. This female carries a packet of eggs which she will soon deposit in the water from which she emerged. That task completed she will die, falling spent with wings outstretched, trapped in the surface film.

BELOW Danica Spinner. With large imitations of floating insects the use of a light, detached body keeps weight to a minimum by using a relatively small hook. In the Danica Spinner, extra floatability comes from a body and wings made of buoyant deerhair.

14

The sherry spinner is the female imago of the blue-winged olive. It exhibits the classic spinner traits of clear, sparkling wings, bright body and elongated tails, all factors which must be reflected in spinner imitations. It ranges in colour from a lobster-pink to a sherry-red, hence the name, and returns to the water to lay its eggs during mid- to late evening.

Spinner imitations are specialized and demand a subtle approach. They must be fine, having either a very light hackle or no hackle at all, and have outstretched wings, suggesting those of the spent spinner, to keep the pattern afloat. Patterns such as the Polywing Spinner or the Sparklewing Spinner can be tied in various sizes, with body colours to mimic the females of the prevailing species.

Sparklewing Spinner. Winding a blue dun hackle through the wings of pearl Twinkle produces a wonderfully lifelike profile of a spent upwing imago or spinner, while the Twinkle adds that clear sparkle typical of the natural's wings. By using this basic design, and by altering hook size and body colour, many different species may be imitated.

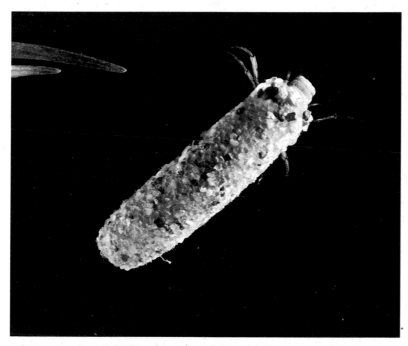

The larvae of many caddis species construct protective cases from sand, small stones or weed cut into pieces. In this specimen the head and legs of the larva can be seen protruding from the case, points which should be included in caddis-larvae imitations.

TRICOPTERA

Caddis-flies, or sedges, belong to the Order Tricoptera. These moth-like insects have a typical roof-winged profile and often very long antennae, which make them readily identifiable. Species range in size from minute micro-caddis at only one-eighth of an inch or so up to 'monsters' such as the great red sedge, *Phryganea grandis*, at almost 1½in. Wing-colour varies, depending on the species, from black to grey, through brown and buff to almost white, and the wings are often heavily mottled. The larger, paler species are usually either nocturnal or emerge only at dusk, while the smaller, darker species are often day-time fliers.

The larvae are aquatic, most building protective homes out of sand, small stones or pieces of cut weed. Some caddis even build cases out of small snail shells, and not always when the snail has finished with them. A number of species, including those of *Hydropsyche* and *Rhyacophila*, are free-swimming for most of their larval stage, building cases only when they pupate. These last forms are the domain of the river angler, with patterns such as Oliver Edwards' Rhyacophila Larva and the Grey Hydropsyche Larva the only imitations you really need.

Imitations of the cased-caddis larvae are more numerous, but among the best are the Peeping Caddis, Van Klinken's Caddis, the Cased Caddis and Grub-head Caddis. Though each is slightly different, all have one thing in common: they carry a good deal of weight.

As the caddis-fly's life-cycle includes a complete metamorphosis, much like a butterfly's or moth's, it must pupate, lying dormant for a period of weeks while its body is 'rearranged'. This goes on within the case, which is sealed by the same tough, chitinous material the larva uses to stick its case together. When fully developed, the pupa uses a pair of jaws, which it sheds as an adult, to bite its way free.

15

Peeping Caddis. Weighted patterns which imitate caddis larva complete with its case are effective in a wide range of water types. On stillwaters, simple leaded patterns work well, while on rivers heavily weighted flies such as the Peeping Caddis are most effective. Here the extra weight, from a split shot, allows the fly to be bumped slowly along the bottom. The body is of dubbed hare's fur, the hackle of brown partridge while the head is of white polypropylene burnt at the end to mimic the larva's head.

Caddis pupae are active creatures able to swim rapidly with the aid of hair-fringed legs which act as paddles. They look like short-winged versions of the adult, though it is still possible to see gills along the sides of the abdomen. This is an amber-bodied type, one of the most common colour varieties.

Caddis pupae are free-swimming creatures with a pair of modified hair-fringed legs which they use as paddles. They come in three basic colours: green, amber and a dirty white, the first two being the most common. Once free of its case, the pupa makes for the surface, where it transposes into the adult either by crawling out on to a dry, bank-side stone or by emerging in open water, right at the surface. The adults of some species actually break free from their pupal shuck beneath the surface, but this is rare.

Of patterns to imitate the sub-surface pupa, few can beat Roman Moser's Ascending Pupa for simplicity and effectiveness. Alternatively, patterns such as the Fur Thorax Caddis Pupa and Gold-head Pupa work well on both still and running water. Imitations of the emerging caddis pupa are also effective when trout are singling out this particular stage, patterns such as the CDC Pupa and the Balloon Caddis being particularly good.

At the surface, the hair-covered wings and body of the adult fly repel water and help it to dry before it becomes airborne. Even so, the caddis often flutters along the surface for a short distance before taking

Fur Thorax Caddis Pupa. Dyed brown rabbit fur, spun in a dubbing loop and then clipped top-and-sides, forms the thorax-hackle for this imitation of an amber-bodied caddis pupa. The pattern may be tied on various sized hooks, from number 8 to 16, and by altering the abdomen colour to either pale green or a dirty off-white all the various species can be imitated.

Adult caddis- or sedge-flies, as they are otherwise known, have a typical roof-winged profile which is a key recognition point. Depending on the species, the wings are usually various shades of brown and are often mottled. Caddis-flies are usually seen around dusk, but some types, especially the smaller, darker species, emerge during the day.

Tierwing Caddis. The high floating property of cul-de-canard is superb for a whole range of dry flies. Here it is the major component of the Tierwing Caddis, where stacks of the feather are layered and then clipped into the profile of an adult caddis fly. The pattern floats beautifully and can be tied either with natural havana cul-de-canard, dyed cinnamon cul-de-canard or, as here, natural grey as a simple silhouette pattern.

18

flight, making a conspicuous disturbance as it does so. Though caddis species exhibit wide variation in colour and size, most trout rises on stillwaters tend to be to the medium-to-large brown or paler species of ½–¾in long. River trout respond readily to hatches of smaller caddis species, particularly early in the season and depending on the preponderance of other insects.

Silhouette and floatability are crucial in adult caddis imitations. Patterns such as the G&H Sedge, the Tierwing Caddis and the Elkhair Caddis fit these criteria superbly.

PLECOPTERA

Members of the Order Plecoptera, or stoneflies, are distinguishable by their hard, heavily veined wings which lie flat over the insect's back when it is at rest. In Britain they range in size from relative giants, such as *Perla bipunctata*, which grows to almost 1¼in to the diminutive needle-flies at only ¼in. The latter are so-called because their wings furl around the body when at rest, giving the insects a slim, needle-like appearance.

Most stoneflies are quite dark, ranging in colour from mid-brown to black, though some, notably the yellow sally, *Chloroperla torrentium*, are bright yellow. Stoneflies are not particularly strong fliers, and when

they do fly, they appear laboured; in fact, in some species the males' wings are so reduced that they are incapable of flight. Other than when the females fly over the water, flopping repeatedly on the surface to lay their eggs, stoneflies seem happier to walk, skulking among bankside stones and vegetation.

The immature stonefly, called the nymph or, sometimes, creeper, is aquatic and in some of the larger species exceptionally long-lived, taking as much as three years to become fully developed. Its preferred habitat is the rocky beds of rain-fed rivers and the rugged shores of large, natural lakes, where it crawls over and beneath rocks and stones. Turn over a submerged rock on one of these waters and you are likely to see a number of these robust, well-camouflaged nymphs, distinguishable from those of upwinged flies by two rather than three tails.

An artificial stonefly nymph, weighted to fish deep in the rough-and-tumble of a rain-fed stream can prove an effective early season tactic. However, in view of the nymph's habit of crawling ashore and transposing into the adult on dry land, emerger patterns are pointless. Any large dark, heavily weighted nymph provides a reasonable representation of a stonefly nymph. Specialist imitations such as Kaufman's Stone, Bird's Stonefly Nymph or the Golden Stone, tied on size 8, 10 and 12 longshank hooks provide more fitting alternatives.

ABOVE Adult stoneflies have hard, shiny, heavily veined wings which lie flat over the abdomen. Some of the smaller species wrap the wings tightly around the body, giving them a slim appearance and the common name of needlefly. Stoneflies are not good fliers and, apart from when the female returns to the water to lay her eggs, are often to be found skulking beneath bankside rocks and leaves.

Adult Stonefly. Grey cul-de-canard forms the wing and hackle of this imitation of an adult stonefly. The pattern can be used to represent the egg-laying female lying spent on the surface, and can be tied in various sizes to imitate a group which ranges in size from the needleflies *Leuctra* sp. at less than ¼in right up to giants such as *Perla bipunctata* at over 1in.

CHIRONOMIDAE

The many species of chironomids or non-biting midges are probably the most important insects of all to fly-fishers. True, on rivers the upwings or olives provide the most noticeable trout rises, but even here the chironomid is important and often the cause of 'impossible' fish. On stillwaters the chironomid's role is unquestionable; it is the number one insect throughout the year.

The adult chironomid is hardly of striking appearance. It isn't very big and species range from minute

Stonefly Nymph. Using a heavy lead underbody, comprising layers of lead foil, allows imitations of the stonefly nymph or 'creeper' to be bumped along the bottom in powerful, swiftly moving water.

BELOW The stonefly nymph, or creeper, is an active creature, clinging to the undersides of submerged rocks in many rain-fed rivers and large natural lakes. It can be distinguished from the nymphs of upwinged species such as the March brown, which share similar habitats, by the fact that it has conspicuous antennae and only two tails instead of the upwing's three.

creatures impossible to imitate on even the smallest hooks up to 'giants' more than ½in long. They vary in colour from black through brown, ginger, olive and green to red, though all have the typical profile of slim abdomen, pronounced thorax and a single pair of wings, the tips falling short of the end of the abdomen. In females of some of the larger species, these wings appear too short for flight, and freshly emerged adults often skim across the surface before becoming airborne.

Identifying individual species in the field is nigh-on impossible, and of little value from an angling viewpoint anyway; size and colour are the important factors. Though males and females of the same species are similar, the males are identifiable by a noticeably slimmer abdomen and more feathery, or plumose, antennae.

What makes the chironomid important is not its size but its sheer numbers. On particularly rich waters the populations are immense, one square metre supporting as many as 100,000 larvae. These are slim, worm-like creatures, varying in size from tiny thread-like

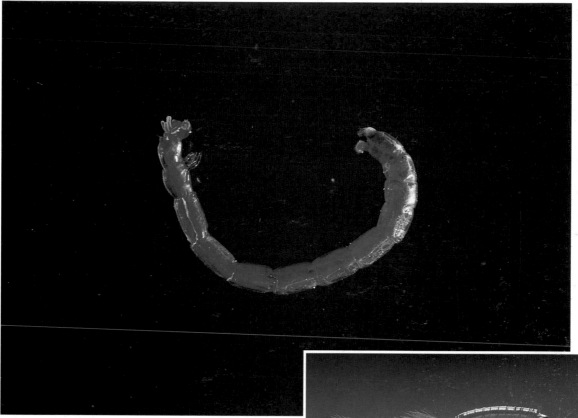

The bright red bloodworm is the most conspicuous and best-known of all the chironomid larvae. It is found in the black silt at the bottom of most lakes and slow-moving rivers. When disturbed it moves with a rapid lashing action of its body, a movement which is difficult to imitate.

Nymph Glass Bloodworm. A short tuft of red marabou is used to mimic the lashing action of the swimming bloodworm.

objects to quite meaty specimens almost ⅜in long. Colour, too, varies. In oxygen-rich habitats green and olive types are abundant, while in the black, oxygen-starved mud on the bed of lakes and slow-moving rivers, red is the colour most widely found. This last is due to the presence of haemoglobin, a chemical with an affinity for oxygen which helps the larvae live in low oxygen levels and is the reason why they are often called bloodworms.

Imitations of the bloodworm are best kept simple. The Ultra Glass Worm is a good example, employing bright red translucent tubing wound over a silver emerger hook. Alternatively, a Silver-head Blood-worm, with its mobile tuft of red marabou for the tail, works well when fished close to the bottom.

Many chironomid larvae build protective tubes from mucous and detritus. There they live and feed, filtering out organic matter from the water. These tubes are also where pupation occurs, a process which takes from a matter of days to weeks depending on the temperature and the time of year. The pupae are quite different from the larvae, having a slim, segmented abdomen, pronounced thorax and white filaments at both head and tail. The wing-buds, too, are noticeable, being located at the sides of the thorax. The colour and size of the pupae vary, but are basically the same as

ABOVE The pupa of the chironomid midge is an extremely important creature for the stillwater fly-fisher, for it forms a large part of the trout's diet. It is taken at all depths, though close to the bottom and right at the surface are the two prime levels.

Ascending Midge Pupa. A strip of pearl lurex running along the back of this midge pupa's abdomen mimics the sparkle created by gases trapped within the skin of the natural insect.

the adult's. If trout are feeding deep down on the pupae, a heavily weighted pattern such as the Epoxy Buzzer or the Wire Buzzer are deadly. Closer to the surface, lighter dressings, such as the True-to-life Buzzer or the Glass Buzzer, tied in a range of colours, are more effective.

When the adult's body has fully developed within the pupal skin, the pupa rises to the surface buoyed up by absorbed gases, which gives it a silvery appearance. At the surface, the pupa hangs with its thorax just through the surface film. Suddenly its body straightens, lying almost parallel to the surface, and the thorax splits open. The adult works its way out of the pupal shuck with a rhythmic pumping action. Then, as the thorax of the adult pulls clear, the wings are pumped with blood, expanding them and giving the emerger a brief, and extremely noticeable, orange flush, an important trigger point in any imitation.

Once free of the spent shuck, the adult chironomid sits on outstretched legs for a moment before taking

ABOVE Just before the pupa transposes into the adult midge, its body straightens so that it lies almost parallel to the water surface. The silvery effect, caused by gas trapped within the pupal skin, is particularly apparent.

RIGHT Blushing Midge. As it emerges from its pupal shuck, the adult midge pumps blood through its wings to expand them. This causes a distinct orange flush which is mimicked in the Blushing Midge with a looped wing bud of dyed orange cul-de-canard.

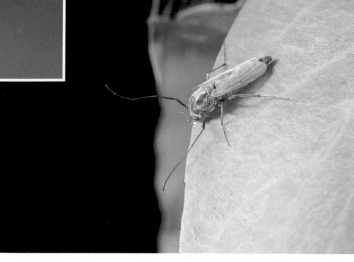

ABOVE Adult Midge. This pattern represents an adult Chironomid midge just after it has emerged from the pupal shuck. Its hackle is clipped beneath the thorax so that it sits low on the water.

RIGHT An adult chironomid midge, identifiable as a female by its small antennae, which lack the feathery, plumose appearance of the male's. Chironomids come in a wide range of colours, from black through to brown and ginger to olive and green. This specimen is olive. Adults are taken either shortly after emergence or when the females return to the water in the evening to lay their eggs.

flight. Eventually great swarms of the males build around the tops of bankside bushes waiting for mates, sometimes a considerable distance from the water. Seen from a distance, these swarms appear like curls of smoke, though the high-pitched buzzing noise they emit gives the game away, and it is this sound that gives the chironomid its popular name of 'buzzer'. The females join the swarms, pairing off with males before returning, usually at dusk, to lay their eggs in gelatinous masses on the water's surface.

The emerging buzzer is a crucial stage for the trout, for the angler and for the insect itself. Imitations must fish right in the surface film; patterns such as the Suspender Buzzer, the Shuttlecock and the Blushing Midge, the latter two using the properties of *cul-de-canard* feathers to keep them at the perfect level. Adult chironomids are less important, though the females returning to lay their eggs can induce a good rise as the evening light fades. A dry midge such as Charles Jardine's excellent Hare's-face Midge or a Poly-midge tied in a variety of colours is seldom found wanting.

DAMSELS AND DRAGONS

The sight of the brilliant, electric blue damselfly stalking the margins is something to gladden the heart of any stillwater fly-fisher; and not just because of the creature's elegant beauty on the wing. Beneath the surface, it is likely that the trout are feeding on the nymphs.

Damselflies belong to the Order Odonata, one which they share with the closely related dragonflies. The damselfly is generally slimmer and smaller than the dragonfly, holding its wings together when at rest, while the dragonfly keeps them spread apart. Taxonomically they are similar, but are divided into suborders, the damselfly being Zygoptera, while the dragonfly is Anisoptera. What is really important is that trout eat the naturals.

Damselflies are creatures of summer. They begin to appear during the latter half of May, and for the fly-fisher this is an indication that he, or she, should look out for trout feeding on the nymphs. The damselfly nymph is aquatic, and for much of its development remains concealed among weed-fronds, using its natural camouflage to disguise it from predators. It feeds on smaller invertebrates, using a wicked hinged

The common blue damselfly makes a wonderful sight as it skims low along the margins of lakes and ponds or perches among bankside vegetation. Only the males of this species are brightly coloured. The females are a greenish-grey. However, the males are sometimes so abundant that the margins seem to be tinged electric blue.

device, known as the labium, to grasp its prey. The nymph of species such as the common blue, *Enallagma cyathigera*, is about 1in long when fully developed, with a long, slim abdomen tipped with three leaf-like gills. Its colour varies according to habitat, ranging

ABOVE This is the typical colour and profile of most damselfly nymphs. They are almost 1in long when mature, with a long, slim body and three distinct leaf-shaped gills, though they sometimes lose one or more of these. Their movements are usually slow and deliberate, but a lashing of the abdomen propels the nymph rapidly when necessary.

Flashback Damselfly Nymph. Pearl lurex and pearl bead eyes contrast with the dull olive if the abdomen and thorax to suggest the mature damsel nymph immediately prior to leaving the water to transpose into the adult.

from a light, almost fluorescent, green to black, with medium olive seemingly the most common.

Although damselfly nymphs are in the water for most of their lives, it is only just before their change into adults that they become important to both fish and fisher. Damselfly nymphs must crawl on to dry land to transpose, and to do this they must quit the relative sanctuary of their weedy homes and move into open water. Gone are the stealthy movements they used to stalk their prey, replaced by a rapid lashing of abdomen and gills which propels them at quite a rate.

Trout, cruising the weed-beds from which the nymphs break cover, mop them up as they swim toward the shore. The fact that the nymphs are counted in their thousands, that they are large, and that they emerge during daylight means that the trout can become heavily preoccupied which means, in turn, that the fly-fisher needs a good imitation if he is going to fool the trout. Damselfly imitations should always be slim with plenty of action – just like the real thing. A tail or body of dyed olive marabou works beautifully, and patterns such as the Flashback Damselfly Nymph, and Marabou-tailed Damsel are deadly.

Once the damselfly nymph has reached dry land, it finds a convenient perch before the adult emerges though a split in the top of the thorax. After half-an-hour or so the freshly emerged adult has dried sufficiently to take flight, though it takes a while longer for the bright blue or red hues of the adult male to reach their full, sparkling brilliance. The female damselfly is generally a duller creature, often a greyish-olive, a fact easily recognized when you see the mating pairs.

Damselfly nymphs leave the water before transforming into the adult stage. Usually they either crawl ashore or up a convenient reed-stem before beginning the process. Then, once the winged stage is clear of the nymphal skin, the fly pumps up its wings and body before sitting still while it dries enough to allow flight. It is some time before the fly darkens to its final colour.

The male and female remain embraced until the female has laid her eggs. The only exception is when the male releases her as she clambers down to deposit eggs on underwater stems. Even then he will grab her as soon as she bobs back to the surface. Trout take adults occasionally, either as they skim over the water's surface or when they are spent. The rise-form of a trout taking a damsel on the wing is spectacular, the fish leaping to take the fly in mid-air. The blue male is imitated by using a detached-bodied dry-fly pattern using deerhair for extra buoyancy. The female, being duller, can be imitated, at a pinch, by a dry Daddy-long-legs.

Though the dragonfly has a similar life-style to that of the damselfly, because it is much less abundant, at least in Britain, it is of relatively little value to the fly-fisher. The nymphs of the largest dragonfly species are big, as much as 2in long, and highly predatory, being capable of tackling even small fish. Not only are they generally larger, but dragonfly nymphs are also much bulkier than those of the damselfly. Their mode of locomotion is also different. They are able to squirt water at pressure from the tip of the abdomen, and this jet-propulsion enables them to move extremely quickly when disturbed.

Dragonfly nymphs are taken by the trout, but because their numbers are much smaller than those of the damselfly, they never elicit a definite feeding pattern. An artificial such as the Lead-eye Dragon, imitating a large bottom-crawling nymph, certainly catches fish, something which cannot be said for imitations of the adult dragonfly.

LEFT Adult Blue Damsel. Dyed blue deerhair is used to create the detached body of this adult damselfly imitation. A detached body means a smaller, lighter hook can be used, increasing the pattern's floatability.

The adult damselfly is a superb, sparkling insect, identifiable from the dragonfly by its two pairs of wings of equal length which are held together when at rest; those of the dragonfly are shorter at the rear and held apart. Trout sometimes take the adult damsel in a spectacular leaping rise as it skims low over the surface.

The dragonfly nymph. Though related to the damselfly nymph, it is much larger and more robust, lacking the three gills at the abdominal tip. Beautifully camouflaged, it is a fierce predator and in the larger species, which grow to 2in or more, it even tackles small fish, grabbing its prey with hinged pincers known as the labium.

Lead Eye Dragon. When trout feed on the nymphs of the dragonfly, patterns such as this lead-eyed imitation can be deadly. Using a small lead dumb-bell to help the fly sink allows it to be fished along the lake bottom around sunken trees and the fringes of weed beds.

CRUSTACEA AND BUGS

The most commonly found crustaceans in trout autopsies are *Gammarus*, often called freshwater shrimps or scud, and the hog-louse, *Asellus*. The various species of each of these creatures are all similar enough to be imitated by the same patterns.

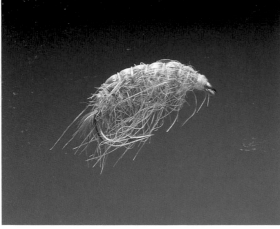

TOP The freshwater shrimp (*Gammarus*) is not a true shrimp but an Amphipod. It is found in many rivers and stillwaters, but prefers a rich alkaline habitat and occurs in greatest profusion in chalk streams and in lakes with a limestone content. At rest it lies in this typical hunchbacked profile, straightening out when it needs to swim quickly. Colours vary, but various shades of olive are the most common. Mating pairs are often seen with the males carrying the females beneath them.

BOTTOM Shrimp. Like many imitations of the freshwater shrimp *Gammarus*, this pattern is tied on a curved shank hook and carries plenty of lead in the underbody to ensure that it sinks quickly. A blend of olive, grey and orange Antron dubbing is used to produce the translucent effect.

The various species of both *Gammarus* and a closely related family, *Crangonyx*, are bottom-dwellers, living among rocks and weed on the bed of the lake or river. They are found in a wide range of waters, from rain-fed rivers through to chalk streams and big lakes, where at times, especially early in the season, they form a substantial part of the trout's diet. They range in colour from a pale, washed-out olive through to dark olive. Some are orange-brown particularly when they are breeding.

They range from approximately ¼in to more than ½in in length. *Gammarus* have only one stage, the young being merely smaller versions of the adults, though they seldom appear in trout autopsies. Their shape at rest is the typical hunchbacked profile, though they straighten their bodies when swimming quickly.

This hunched profile of the freshwater shrimp is fortuitous, allowing its imitations to be packed full of lead to make them sink quickly without producing excessive bulk. So when trout are feeding deep, often on natural shrimps, an artificial can be fished at just the right level. Various patterns, such as the Flexi Shrimp and the Swimming Shrimp, work well.

HOG-LOUSE (*ASELLUS SP*)

This small, drab crustacean inhabits many lakes and slow-moving rivers, where it skulks in bottom detritus

Hoglouse. Hare's fur and brown partridge feather combine to produce this effective imitation of the hoglouse *Asellus*. It is well weighted with lead wire allowing it to be fished slowly along the bottom in the same habitat as the naturals are to be found.

and weed. It is a much poorer swimmer than *gammarus* and occurs less frequently in autopsies. That said, when trout are feeding on the hog-louse, they often do so exclusively. Hog-lice range in colour from a light greyish-brown to almost black, and in length from ¼in to more than ½in.

Few imitations of the hog-louse have been devised, but those which are available often use brown partridge hackles to imitate the natural's legs. At a pinch, a Hare's-ear Nymph, well picked out, can be effective. All hog-louse imitations should be well weighted and fished slowly along the bottom.

CORIXAE

Corixae are small, beetle-like bugs belonging to the Order Hemiptera. They occur in the shallow margins of many lakes and slow-moving rivers, where they feed on decaying plant and animal material. The various species range in length from ¼ to more than ½in, and in colour from a light golden-olive through to brown and almost black. Corixae are not fully aquatic. They have no gills and must return to the surface

The water hog-louse (*Asellus*) is a poor swimmer and is found mainly in slow-moving parts of a river, such as back-eddies, and in lakes and ponds, where it moves through weed-fronds and among decaying leaves. It is often taken by the trout during the early part of the season, March and April, when aquatic insect numbers are low.

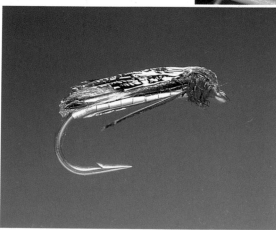

ABOVE Though this small insect looks like a beetle, the corixa belongs to the Order Hemiptera, which includes the closely related backswimmer *Notonecta*. Corixa don't have gills, but fulfil an aquatic existence by means of an 'aqualung', a bubble of air which is obtained at the surface and trapped around the creature's belly like a silvery coat.

Silver Corixa. The Silver Corixa imitates the natural corixa just after it has replenished its air supply from the surface. This bubble of air gives the corixa's body a wonderful silvery appearance which is mimicked by silver lurex in the imitation. An underbody of lead wire running along the sides of the hook shank, rather than being wound, is used to give the pattern a flattened profile and help it sink.

every few minutes to replenish their air supply. This is held wrapped around the underside of the creature's body as a conspicuous, silver bubble. The extra air makes the corixa extremely buoyant, and it must use a pair of hair-fringed legs to paddle itself to the bottom; there it clings to an immovable object, such as a stone or piece of weed, while it feeds.

Corixae imitations are usually tied on size 12 or 14 wet-fly hooks. All are either pale-bodied or use silver tinsel or Mylar to mimic the silver bubble of air held beneath the creature's body. Simple hackled patterns such as the Buff Corixa take a lot of fish, as do more complicated dressings, including the Silver Corixa and the Paddling Corixa, which include imitations of the paddle-like legs of the natural.

SNAILS

Trout which are taking snails exhibit two distinct feeding patterns, each dictated by the habits of the snail itself. The first is a simple browsing technique, the fish picking individual snails from the lake-bed and the weed just as they graze algae. This type of feeding is difficult to predict and often a fish caught on a

standard deep-fished nymph or lure is one that has been 'snailing'. Unfortunately, in such circumstances the logical ploy of using a deep-fished chunky pattern, such as a Black and Peacock Spider, is usually ineffective.

The second type of snail feeding is again difficult to predict, but when it does happen, the use of the right pattern can dramatically affect results. Such feeding occurs when the snails migrate at certain times of year, usually during warm weather. Some species rise to the surface, clinging to the underside of the surface film and travel long distances by their own locomotion and surface drift. Just why they do this is uncertain, but the important thing is that trout may at such times become preoccupied with floating snails. The problem is that this type of feeding is also difficult to identify. The trout go 'wild', are hard to tempt, and nothing is visible at the surface – the snail is just beneath it.

If such a feeding pattern occurs in warm conditions, suspect the snail as the culprit. Have a good look in the margins for floating naturals and, if you find any, try a floating imitation in either black or dark olive, the two most popular colours for the natural. The Foam Snail, which uses closed-cell foam coloured with a Pantone pen, or a clipped deerhair imitation such as

Snails rising to the surface prove a boon for the trout, but the opposite for the fly-fisher. Working out the cause of an 'impossible' rise can be tricky, but if a fish is landed it can be spooned and, if snails are responsible, a relevant imitation presented to the fish. Often you don't need to spoon snail-feeders; the shells within make the fish virtually rattle!

Floating snail. Using deerhair rather than foam for the shell of a floating snail imitation allows the floatation of the pattern to be altered before it is cast out. A gentle squeeze, under the water, will expel some of the air so that the pattern sits just under the surface film, not on top of it.

the Floating Snail, both work well. The point to remember is that the pattern should hang just sub-surface. If it is too buoyant, it will be refused.

DAPHNIA

The tiny water fleas called daphnia certainly make up in numbers what they lack in size, and even in modest-sized waters they can be counted in their millions.

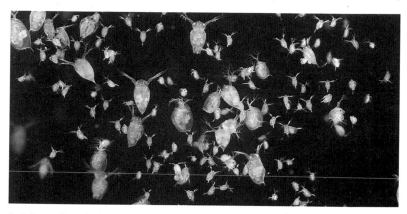

Daphnia are tiny animal plankton with individuals no more than ⅛in long. However, the fact that they occur in millions means that they are an important trout food, especially in lakes and reservoirs. The technique of trout feeding on daphnia is simple: they swim through the swarms, mouths open, taking in great gulps of the living soup.

The great swarms don't go unnoticed by the trout. Rainbows, in particular, are great daphnia-feeders, swimming through the concentrations of this animal plankton and scooping in great mouthfuls. This living soup is highly nutritious, and trout feeding on daphnia rapidly pack on weight and condition.

Although it is impossible to imitate daphnia, it is important to locate the swarms, as this is often where the fish are to be found. Daphnia do not like strong light, and in bright sunshine they migrate into deeper water. This is a critical factor when it comes to finding daphnia feeders, and it pays to experiment with sinking lines of various densities until the correct depth is found. Both lures and wet flies of various colours work well, though patterns with a heavy orange bias are particularly effective.

FISH

Trout, both browns and rainbows, are highly predatory and when the chance of a high-protein meal such

Small fish make up a substantial proportion of the stillwater trout's diet. During late-summer/early autumn in particular, trout hit the shoals of small coarse-fish fry aggressively, forcing the hapless fry to leap clear of the surface in panic. The roach, *Rutilus rutilus*, is probably the most common prey species, followed by the perch and bream.

Deerhair Roach Fry. Deerhair imitations of various coarse fish species, such as the roach, are tremendously effective when trout are hitting the shoals. Using white deerhair spun and then clipped into the shape of a small fish, the resulting pattern can be left plain, as in the Spondoolie, or coloured to match the natural countershading of a real fish. The addition of an eye, either glass or painted on, makes the pattern even more deadly.

as a small fish comes their way, they grab it. However, trout seldom take fish in a haphazard way; indeed, fry-feeders exhibit a range of specific feeding patterns which need to be identified quickly and reliably.

On stillwaters, species such as the perch, roach and bream are the main fodder fish. Though all three species grow much bigger, 1–4in is an optimum size for the trout. Sticklebacks are also taken, particularly on smaller lakes and where other species are absent, but their sharp dorsal and pelvic spines make them a difficult prey for the trout to swallow. The soft, defenceless roach is probably the number one species on larger lakes, and towards the latter part of the season, September and October, they are taken in great numbers. The prey fish's tactic of shoaling is a great defence against predators, but the heavy concentrations that build up in shallow water around weed-beds and boat docks offer the trout a tempting target.

One of the trout's major fry-feeding strategies is to drive headlong into the fry shoals, often returning quickly to mop up the casualties. This occurs both in the margins and in open water, and it is identified by the shoals of small fish scattering in panic across the surface. An ordinary large white streamer can prove effective in such circumstances, though patterns such as the Appetizer (which mimics more closely the coloration of a small fish) are a better choice. A big, grey Rabbit

Zonker may also work well, and the Minkie, with its highly mobile wing of mink strip, is deadly when fished slowly through areas of activity. Tandems and tube-flies are also effective, especially when fished from a boat, and particularly the all-tinsel types such as the Pulsar. Choose a pattern which is roughly the same size as the prey species being taken. This is as important as choosing the right pattern, though it can mean tying on a fly of 4in or even 5in in length.

Other feeding strategies include the picking-off of natural mortalities. Small, shoaling fish, especially perch, are prone to disease, and when sudden die-offs occur, trout often cruise the weed-beds, picking off the dead and dying. This method of feeding is often quite gentle, a far cry from the commotion of a straight drive. Instead, the trout pick the small dead fish off the surface, often producing a dimple rise-form more in keeping with that of buzzer feeding.

Patterns designed to float on the surface are deadly when trout are feeding this way. Often nothing more than an Ethafoam Doll or Mylar Fry is needed, though a deerhair fry such as the Spondoolie will outfish virtually any other pattern when the fish are really selective. The reason patterns of this type are so deadly is that the buoyancy of the deerhair can be balanced with the weight of the hook to produce a fly which floats just under the surface – exactly as the natural does.

Coarse-fish fry have a high mortality rate and many die through disease. Often they float to the surface, lying on their sides, and trout cruise the edges of weed-beds picking off individual fry with a gentle rise more in keeping with that of buzzer feeders. Don't be fooled. In these circumstances a small floating fry can be absolutely deadly.

Another major feeding pattern occurs much earlier in the season, only a few weeks after the young fish have hatched. Often no more than ¼–½in long, these tiny fry are very thin and quite transparent, earning them the nickname of needle-fry. Trout which target this particular stage can be difficult to fool, and even identifying this food-source can be tricky as the fry are rapidly digested and all a spooning reveals is a grey soup containing a few small spines.

Imitating the needle-fry is equally difficult, and a task made no easier by the vast numbers of the genuine article. Trout move through the shoals, mouths open, scooping in the hapless individuals as they go. Small, translucent patterns such as the Pearl Fry, Rabbit Fry and Sinfoil's Fry catch fish, though, curiously, a small dry fly is often the best ploy.

River trout, especially browns in the less rich rainfed rivers, where other forms of life are not so prolific, also take fish. The sedentary bullhead or miller's thumb, is a favourite, though stone loaches are also

33

LEFT Deerhair Sculpin. Brown trout, especially the larger specimens, are extremely predatory. On both lakes and rivers an imitation of a small fish such as miller's thumb or sculpin can tempt trout of a size not normally fooled by smaller nymph and dry fly patterns. The Deerhair Sculpin uses a muddler head in conjunction with a highly mobile tail of rabbit or mink fur strip to deadly effect.

BELOW Trout take fish in rivers as well as in lakes. One of the most common prey species is the bullhead, or miller's thumb. Early in the season it is not unknown for even a modest-sized brown trout to be caught which has the tail of a bullhead sticking out of its throat.

taken. Though seldom used on British rivers, at least for ordinary brown trout, streamer patterns can work well in such situations. Imitations of the bullhead are also effective, tempting the bigger specimen trout which many rivers hold, but which usually ignore small nymphs and dry flies.

Imitations of the bullhead range from a large standard Muddler Minnow, originally designed to imitate a fish not unlike a bullhead, to a large brown Zonker. A specific imitation such as Oliver Edwards' Sculpin hairy or the Deerhair Sculpin also work well; both should be about 2in long, well weighted to combat the buoyancy of the deerhair head, and fished close to the bottom.

TERRESTRIALS

Much of what the trout eats is not aquatic but consists of land creatures which fall or are blown into the water. Various flies, beetles and spiders plus, from time to time, ants and grasshoppers are usually covered by the catch-all title of 'terrestrials'. Throughout the year, as the populations of these various creatures reach their peak, they may end up on the water in sufficient quantities for the trout to feed on them specifically. Such an event demands a reasonable imitation.

THE CRANEFLY

Perhaps the best-known terrestrial is the cranefly, or daddy-long-legs. The various species of this large, gangling insect occur throughout the summer, but particularly large hatches are seen towards autumn, when the weather is usually cooler and damper. Although some species of cranefly have aquatic larval and pupal stages, it is the more numerous and fully terrestrial species which are most important to the angler. Their larvae live in the grassy banks and waterside fields of lakes and rivers. These grey, legless grubs – leatherjackets – are the creatures which are the bane of gardeners everywhere, destroying the roots of their prize plants.

Once fully grown, the larva pupates and the adult which emerges is the large, spindly-legged creature attracted to our house-lights on damp autumn nights. The daddy is not a strong flier, and in a good offshore breeze is easily blown over the water. At first its legs are capable of supporting it and it is able to land on and take flight from the water a number of times as it

careers downwind. Eventually, though, it becomes swamped, trapped in the surface film from which there is no escape.

Good falls of daddies bring dramatic rises, though they are sometimes slow to start. Daddy-long-legs are big insects; the body of a large female is more than 1in long and the six long legs make it look even larger. The size seems to put off the fish initially, and for a few days it may be possible to watch countless naturals bounce along on the ripple with hardly a rise to be seen.

But when the trout do finally cotton on, the rise can be spectacular, and each insect which hits the surface is met with a hefty swirl. On many lakes, from lowland

The cranefly or daddy-long-legs, *Tipula* spp, is at its peak during the cooler, damper weeks of late August and September. These terrestrial insects are weak fliers and are easily blown on to the water by a strong offshore breeze. Trout may take a while to tune in to such a large insect, but patterns which imitate the long, straggly legs and slim tapering abdomen are effective once they do.

reservoirs to the rich limestone loughs of Ireland, the daddy has the reputation of tempting the bigger fish. Often it is a dry imitation daddy which fools the best fish of the season, especially on natural waters – and these are often great brawling trout weighing more than 10lb.

Many daddy-long-legs imitations are available, tied either as wet or dry flies. Because an imitation needs to be large, detached bodies are effective for dry-fly versions. These use a buoyant material, such as deer-hair or foam, to form the body, allowing a smaller, lighter hook to be used than if the pattern were tied directly on to a longshank hook. Two fine patterns of

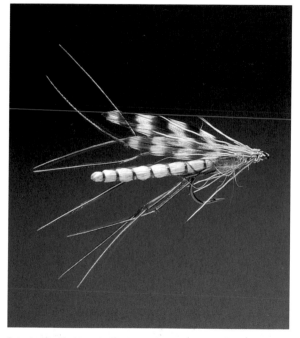

Detached Daddy. Natural elk hair is used to form a light detached body for this imitation of the cranefly or daddy longlegs. Knotted fibres of cock pheasant tail mimic the gangling legs of the natural.

this type are the Deerhair Daddy and the Detached Daddy. The main point to remember is to mimic the long legs, an important recognition point for the trout. They can be tied from lengths of brown nylon or cock pheasant tail-fibres, each knotted twice to suggest the joints. Weight is not such a problem with wet versions, and any pattern such as the Hackled Daddy and Walker's Cranefly will catch fish provided they mimic the gangling, leggy effect of a drowned natural.

HAWTHORN AND HEATHER FLIES

Many species of terrestrial flies find their way on to the water's surface throughout the season, but few cause the trout to react as dramatically as does the hawthorn fly, *Bibio marci*. It is related to the back gnat, *Bibio johannis*, but has a more specific season, from about the end of April to the second week in May.

The male is easily identifiable, being black and quite large, about ½in long, with big, bulbous eyes, and long trailing back legs. The female resembles a large

TOP Towards the end of April and into the first weeks of May, the males of the hawthorn fly can be seen dancing in swarms above bushes, notably hawthorns in full bloom. Because of this, it is usually the males, which have long, trailing back-legs, which end up on the water. Of the two sexes this is the one to imitate.

BOTTOM Foam Hawthorn Fly. Foam and deerhair are used to form the thorax head and hackle of this terrestrial imitation. The use of a detached body also helps to create a lifelike pattern which floats right in the surface film.

black gnat, lacking the male's long legs. The males swarm around bankside vegetation, often around flowering hawthorn bushes, on the look-out for females, and they are easily blown over the water in a strong breeze. If they land on the water, they quickly become incapacitated, and an easy target for surface-feeding trout. But as with the daddy-long-legs, trout do take a while to become accustomed to eating them.

A rise to naturals can be dramatic and sustained for as long as the flies keep coming. Standard dry-fly tactics work, but a good imitation is needed, particularly during a large fall. The fish become quite selective, and a pattern which floats in the surface film and which possesses those all-important trailing legs can make the difference. The Foam Hawthorn is just such a fly, effective on both still and running water.

A related species, the heather fly, *Bibio pomonae*, is an insect of the heather and most often found around lochs and lakes in Scotland, Wales and northern England. Similar in size and shape to the hawthorn fly, the adults have distinctive red-coloured leg joints, which are the probable reason for the design of the Bibio wet-fly with its red-centred black body. Falls of heather fly are less prolific than those of the hawthorn, but in the usually poorer environment, opportunist trout are quick to take advantage. A Bibio is a first choice, but a Hawthorn with red legs makes a suitable alternative.

HOVERFLIES

Hoverflies are small, wasp-like insects, abundant from mid- to late summer and often confused with droneflies, which are related but are usually larger and darker, resembling male honey-bees or drones. Hoverflies frequently fall on to the water in significant numbers, especially the larger stillwaters, and then a good imitation is important. Points to mimic are the amber- and black-banded body and the red eyes, which are pronounced on freshly emerged specimens. The larvae of hoverflies feed on aphids or greenflies, and their numbers are governed by their prey's abundance. So when you find your garden plagued with greenfly, you can at least look forward to a good fall of hoverflies a few weeks later.

Find heather and often you will find the heather fly, a relative of the hawthorn fly. Though not as numerous, the heather fly has striking red joints to its legs, and imitations should reflect this colour variation.

ABOVE Large falls of the small terrestrial hoverfly are common during the heat of summer, especially on the larger man-made lakes. At first glance, the hoverfly looks like a small wasp, with its striking black- and amber-banded abdomen. However, close examination reveals only a single pair of wings, which means that the fly belongs to the Order Diptera, the same as craneflies and chironomids, and is totally harmless.

Hover Fly. Using closed cell foam for the body of this hover or drone fly imitation produces a pattern which will float all day but which sits right in the surface film like a frowning natural.

BEETLES

Although aquatic beetles are numerous, it is the terrestrial species which are of greatest interest to the trout angler. They range from minute black pollen beetles, imitations of which need to be dressed on size 22 hooks, up to the meaty June bug, a relative of the cockchafer. This particular beetle, *Phyllopertha* *horticola*, is otherwise known as the coch-y-bondhu, a creature of almost mythical proportions in Wales and seemingly capable of attracting virtually every fish in a lake. The natural is about ½in long with reddish-brown wing-covers and a metallic greenish-blue head, and during June and early July it swarms in vast numbers, certainly enough to elicit a substantial rise.

Various traditional imitations exist of this insect, but a brown Foam Beetle, which sits right in the surface film, is effective. Using closed-cell foam of varying colours to produce buoyancy and a beetle shape is an effective technique and can be modified to imitate a wide range of species. Deerhair may also be used, but it is not so robust.

GRASSHOPPERS

Grasshoppers are less important on stillwaters than on rivers, where a quick leap in the wrong direction can see these large, meaty creatures at the mercy of the current and a finning trout. 'Hopper days' are few and far between in Britain and occur only during mid- to late summer, when the naturals are most active. On hot, sultry afternoons, with little activity, a few deft swipes of the landing-net in bankside vegetation can lead to a 'surprise' hopper fall. Then it pays to try one of the specialist patterns such as Dave's Hopper or, failing that, a small Brown Muddler.

TOP Dave's Hopper.

BOTTOM Thanks to pesticides and other aspects of land management, grasshoppers are not as numerous as they were. However, when a summer sun beats down and the surface of the river is unmarked by rising fish, the heavy plop of a 'hopper' can interest even the most lethargic trout.

38

TYPES OF FLY

The artificial fly is intrinsic to the art of fly-fishing. Tackle and technique may be perfect, but it is all for nought if the fly being used is unacceptable to the trout.

Fly-fishing has come a long way since those Macedonian anglers fashioned feather and wool and cast for speckled skinned fish living in streams. But however advanced we think we have become, we still have much in common with our ancestors. Foremost is the satisfaction of mimicking the colour and form of a natural insect and fooling the trout into taking it. Although pattern types have developed dramatically in shape, size and action, the underlying premise of identifying the food-form on which the trout are feeding and producing an artificial to match is as relevant today as it ever was.

The artificials those earliest fly-fishers used seem to have been basically dry or dapped flies. Today we use flies which break down into four main classifications: dry, wet, nymph and lure. Within each is a rich and diverse array of patterns and types, not all of which fit perfectly into a specific group, but sufficiently so to give a guide as to their basic shape and how they should be fished.

THE DRY FLY

As its name suggests, a dry fly should float and not sink and become wet. Dry flies were originally developed on running water, ostensibly to imitate the imago and sub-imago stages of various upwing and Mayfly species. As such, the standard upwing profile, with paired, erect wings and a tail and a hackle to keep it afloat, became the norm. The problem was that in running water the hackle quickly became sodden and the fly sank. This was counteracted by the use of steely, sharp-fibred cock hackles which, being stiff and non-absorbent, kept the fly floating for much longer. So the quest for the glossy, high-grade cock cape began, in rich glowing colours from natural red game to Greenwell, honey, blue-dun and the wonderful speckling of grizzle.

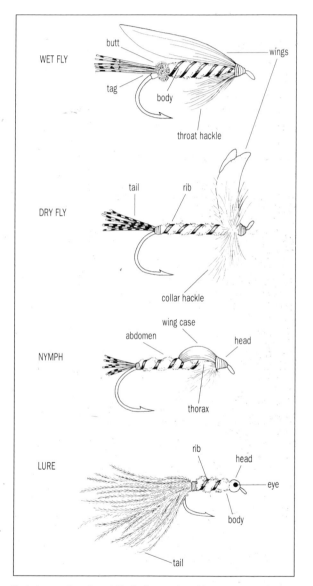

Typical proportions for wet fly, dry fly, nymph and lure.

Today we are more fortunate. Modern flotants, used for proofing flies before they are cast, repel water superbly, and even a fly which has become waterlogged, or which has just caught a trout, is up and floating after a few false casts. This has opened up a whole new range of materials which can be used for tying dry flies, and the art of imitative fly-tying has moved significantly forward. Flotants are now so efficient that flies can be tied very sparsely or entirely without hackles, relying on teased-out body materials or strategically placed wings to keep them in the surface film.

We now have the means to tie slim, delicate dry flies much closer in form to natural insects, without recourse to great, bushy hackles. But however much we crave, stiff, glossy hackles for our dry flies, the creatures we imitate with them are often neither. Most freshly hatched duns are delicate and matt, so a soft, dull hackle which collapses as the fish takes it surely produces a more convincing imitation.

TRADITIONAL DRY FLIES

It was the late nineteenth and early twentieth centuries which saw the development of what we now know as the traditional dry fly. Its profile became stereotyped, typically with paired, upright wings, body, tail, plus a stiff-fibred collar hackle which kept the whole affair afloat. Patterns such as the Red Quill, Adams, Light Cahill, Blue-winged Olive, Gold-ribbed Hare's Ear and Greenwell's Glory, which are now deeply embedded in fly-fishing lore, were designed principally to imitate the duns and sometimes spinners of various species of ephemeroptera. This stereotyping became so ingrained that even some caddis patterns were tied with upright paired wings whereas the natural has a roof-winged profile.

As an imitation of an upwinged fly, the standard dry fly is still an effective style. Patterns such as the Adams and Gold-ribbed Hare's Ear remain excellent fish-catchers, used either during a specific insect hatch or speculatively when fish are rising to nothing in particular. That said, fly-fishers are always keen to develop evermore effective and lifelike imitations, so the basic dry-fly profile has been manipulated to produce a wide range of variations designed to cope with differing conditions.

SIMPLE HACKLED DRY FLIES

The hackled dry fly is probably the most widely used. Its main attribute is that it is simple and quick to tie, making it ideal for most dry-fly patterns, particularly

The Grey Duster is a simple hackled dry fly which imitates nothing in particular. This is the key to its effectiveness for it is a deadly fly on both running and still waters when fish are feeding non-specifically. However, it works particularly well when tied in its smaller sizes on size 16–20 hooks during a hatch of chironomid midge or the smaller, lighter upwings.

those used when fish are feeding non-specifically. While many of us would like to believe that close imitation is the key, realistically, a more general pattern, suggestive of something edible to the fish, is quite enough to fool most into taking. It is a role that the hackled dry fly fulfils superbly.

Simple, hackled patterns, without wings, work well in water conditions as varied as the broken tumble of a rocky stream, the smooth glide of a chalk stream, and the glassy calm of an unruffled lake surface. They are versatile imitators and may be used to suggest a whole wealth of creatures, both aquatic and terrestrial, from beetles and spiders to upwing flies and caddis; virtually anything which might find itself trapped in the water's surface film. They have a long history, too. Patterns such as the Grey Duster, Coch-y-Bondhu, Red Tag, and Tup's Indispensable have been taking fish for more years than anyone dare remember.

Most dry flies can be tied in this simple collar style, where the hackle is wound as a ruff just behind the hook eye. Various coloured hackles may be used, including natural red game, ginger, blue dun, greenwell and black through to grizzle. Some wonderful and effective mottled variants can be produced by mixing, for example, red game and grizzle or black and grizzle.

PARACHUTE-HACKLED DRY FLIES

One early dry-fly variation was the Parachute hackle. Here, rather than being tied around the hook, the hackle is wound around a small, upright post on the hookshank so that it sits in the same plane as the shank. As all the hackle-fibres potentially work on the water's surface, fewer are needed to keep the fly afloat, which allows for a more sparse, lifelike effect. Also, because the hackle is entirely above the hook, the body of the fly sits low, or may even project below the surface. This makes the Parachute a superb style for tying patterns which mimic an upwing, a midge, or even a caddis-fly at the point of emergence.

Virtually any dry-fly pattern may be tied in Parachute style, but a number of highly effective dressings have been developed specifically as Parachutes. Among the most popular is the Paradun series, which is tied in a variety of sizes and shades to mimic any upwinged species. Other patterns include The Gulper and the Klinkhammer Special, the latter being a devastatingly effective catcher of grayling when fished in broken water. All three use wing posts of polypropylene, a man-made, water-repellent material which is not only a great support for the hackle but doubles as a sight indicator, helping the angler to see takes when the fly is sitting low in the water.

THORAX-TIE

Another effective style that can be used for hackling dry flies, especially those which imitate the dun or sub-imago of an upwinged fly, is the thorax-tie. The hackle is wound round the hook-shank as in the traditional dry fly, but rather than the turns being closely butted together, they are spread to cover the whole thoracic area. This makes the hackle-fibres more efficient, and because they are spread similarly to the legs of the natural, they produce a more lifelike 'footprint' on the surface.

It is the way in which the hackle-fibres dent the surface which forms a recognition point for the fish and makes the thorax-tie a deadly dun imitation for difficult or 'educated' trout. The 'footprint' may be improved further by clipping the hackle short, not flush, just beneath the hook-shank. Only a small section should be removed, so that the remaining hackle-fibres, projecting below the hook, form a shallow, inverted 'V'. This trimming not only reduces hackle

bulk without reducing flotation, but gives a more lifelike profile and ensures that the fly alights the correct way up more than 80 per cent of the time.

Because of the extremely lifelike profile, thorax-tie patterns are equally effective on both still and running water. Indeed, one of the most killing of all dun imitations is the Cul-de-canard Dun, which uses a feather taken from around a duck's preen gland for the wing. In their natural state, *cul-de-canard* feathers are oily and water repellent, while retaining a wonderful delicacy which makes them ideal for imitating the diaphanous wing of the real dun. Add to this the fact that CDC feathers come in a range of greys similar in shade to those of upwing duns and one realizes what a great contribution they have made to imitative fly-tying.

NO-HACKLE DRY FLIES

In calm, difficult conditions, or when fishing for educated trout, ordinary hackled patterns may be totally ignored. Back in the 1960s the Americans Carl Richards and Doug Swisher produced a range of no-hackle patterns designed to fool those trout which might otherwise be considered impossibly selective. One of their most enduring innovations has been the Compara-dun series, a range of flies tied to imitate

Using a flared collar of deer body hair for support, rather than a standard cock hackle, the Compara-dun floats well even in broken water. It was devised by American duo Al Caucci and Bob Nastasi to give a lifelike imitation of a freshly hatched upwing dun.

41

42

freshly emerged duns. Using merely a flared wing and tails to keep the fly afloat, the Compara-dun may be tied in a variety of body colours and on a wide range of hook-sizes to imitate any species of upwing dun.

The original Compara-dun uses the buoyant properties of deerhair for both wing and tail. Flaring the tips of the hair 180 degrees around the top and sides of the thorax creates a really lifelike profile, while the tips of the hair, at the sides, catch in the surface film and keep the fly afloat. While deerhair works well, polypropylene yarn can be used instead. Although the poly-wing is more clinical in its profile, the superb water-resistant properties of polypropylene, especially the siliconized type, make for a fly which floats all day long, even after catching many fish.

One further modification which can be effective is to substitute clear Antron or poly yarn, for the deerhair tail. The resultant Sparkle Dun, with its sparkling tail, imitates an upwing dun at the very moment it is has pulled free from its nymphal shuck. It is a deadly pattern for many river and stillwater applications.

STILLWATER DRY FLIES

Whereas the bulk of river-based dry flies are imitations of either ephemerids or caddis-flies, those used on stillwaters are usually imitations of the chironomid midge. The reason is simple: the chironomid makes up a large proportion of the stillwater trout's diet. For the dry-fly angler it is the adult midge which is the target stage, and patterns tied to represent this insect come in a wide range of sizes and colours, reflecting the diversity of the natural.

The adult midge emerges from its pupal shuck and sits low on the water's surface before taking flight. Imitations are presented in the same manner and are designed to fish on or just in the surface film. They are tied sparse, either with no hackle at all or with just a turn or two to give balance and help them float. Patterns tied in this format include the Carrot Fly, the Poly-winged Midge, the Elk-hair Midge and the Hare's-face Midge. Although many stillwater dry flies have a wing, often it is nothing more than a 'sighter', allowing the angler to see the fly at long range.

The other major style of tying typical of the stillwater dry fly is the Hopper. Don't confuse this fly with an imitation of a grasshopper. It bears no resemblance. The Hopper has six, trailing legs, fashioned from knotted, cock pheasant tail-fibres. These, and the low level at which the Hopper sits on the surface, produce a 'busy' profile and are the key to its success.

While the Hopper may look like an imitation of a small daddy-long-legs, it is effective throughout the season, even when no daddies are on the water. Regarded as a general dry-fly pattern, it is devastatingly effective either when cast to rising fish or for tempting fish 'out of the blue'. The Hopper is usually tied on a size 12 or 14 long-shanked hook in colours ranging from orange to green, red and black. An amber version with a pearl Lurex rib is especially deadly.

EMERGERS

Emergers are designed to imitate the transition of an aquatic nymph or pupa into the winged adult. With those insect types which emerge in open water, such as many upwinged flies, caddis-flies and chironomid midges, it is an important target stage for the fish. Emerging aquatic insects are extremely vulnerable to predators. As nymphs and larvae they remain concealed among weeds or in the bottom silt; as adults they are able to fly away. But as emergers they are trapped for a time in limbo, right in the surface film, with each insect totally at the mercy of feeding fish until it pulls free from its shuck.

Most emerger imitations reflect this halfway stage and are tied so that the thorax and emerging wings float on the surface while the abdomen hangs beneath, mimicking the profile of the natural nymphal or pupal shuck. Buoyant materials such as deerhair, microcellular foam, polypropylene and cul-de-canard feathers all work well for the floating, thoracic section. They should be tied to project upwards and sideways to suggest the winged adult breaking free and to gain maximum hold in the water's surface.

More absorbent materials are used for the abdomen. Various types of dubbing and feather fibre work well, as do some of the finer plastic strips. In fact, any material which works well for normal, lightweight, nymph and pupa imitations does equally well for an emerger. Effective emerger patterns for the caddis include Moser's Emerging Pupa, the Balloon Caddis and the Emerging Caddis; for upwings, the Emerging Ephemerid, the Mayfly Emerger and the CDC Emerger; and for the midge, the Shuttlecock, the Deerhair Emerger and Shipman's Buzzer tied in a variety of colours.

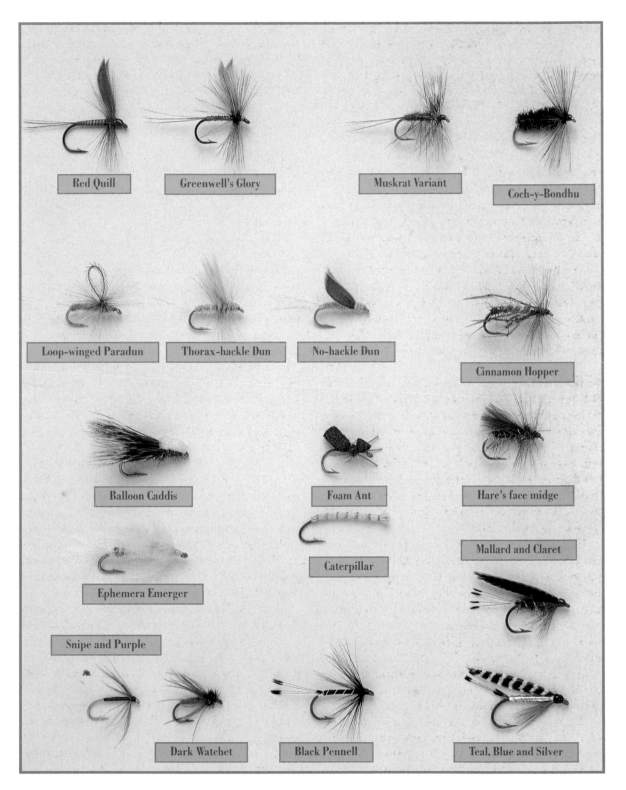

Red Quill

Greenwell's Glory

Muskrat Variant

Coch-y-Bondhu

Loop-winged Paradun

Thorax-hackle Dun

No-hackle Dun

Cinnamon Hopper

Balloon Caddis

Foam Ant

Hare's face midge

Caterpillar

Mallard and Claret

Ephemera Emerger

Snipe and Purple

Dark Watchet

Black Pennell

Teal, Blue and Silver

44

Austria's Roman Moser is fast gaining a reputation as one of Europe's most accomplished fly-fishers and innovative fly tiers; any pattern which he invents is worth a second look. Roman's flies are usually developed for a specific purpose and this simple but effective Emerging Caddis Pupae was designed to imitate those found on his native River Traun.

TERRESTRIALS

Another major group of dry flies is that which imitates the terrestrials. These include creatures such as grasshoppers, spiders, beetles, ants, hawthorn flies and daddy-long-legs; in fact, any small, non-aquatic, invertebrate which becomes trapped on the water surface.

Many can be encompassed within other dry-fly groups, but others, such as beetles and grasshoppers, are so different from the aquatic insects we usually imitate, that they need a different form of imitation.

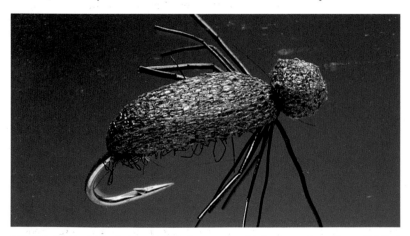

Using fine closed-cell foam for terrestrial imitations, such as this beetle, creates patterns which float just in the surface film but which require no floatant. The key is to balance the amount of foam used with the weight of the hook so that the fly sits very low in the water.

Unusual materials are often used to create the correct profile. Grasshoppers, for instance, are big and bulky and best imitated by using a Muddler technique more often associated with tying lures.

Here the deerhair is spun and clipped to the shape of the grasshopper's head. Effective beetle patterns may also be produced from deerhair, but instead of being spun, it it is tied over the back of the hook to produce the typical shell-back profile. Using deerhair rather than foam produces an imitation which sits just under the surface in exactly the same manner as the natural.

THE WET FLY

The flip side of the dry fly is the wet fly, designed to sink quickly and to fish sub-surface. The term wet fly covers a diverse range of pattern styles, from simple hackled flies to patterns with intricate wings and body hackles, but as long as they are intended to fish beneath the surface, they are considered wet flies.

SPIDERS AND SOFT-HACKLE FLIES

Most basic of all wet flies are the spider and the soft-hackle patterns. They have a long tradition and have been used widely for catching trout and grayling almost as long as man has fly-fished.

Though often called spiders, these flies are not intended to be spider imitations. It is their simple, sparse hackle which gives them their spider-like appearance; hence the name. In practice, this mobile hackle suggests the legs of a small nymph or a drowned insect, which in the rough-and-tumble of a rain-fed stream is more than adequate to fool a trout. However, this doesn't mean that spiders are in any way second-best to more specific imitations.

Their simplicity and the fact that they may be tied extremely delicately means that spiders often fool fish which have already seen imitative patterns. When trout are feeding on tiny midges or smuts, or any of the smaller ephemerids, such as the iron blue, a small

Black Spider can be deadly. 'Small', can be interpreted as a size 16, 18 or even a size 20.

The hallmark of a good spider pattern is a sparse, mobile hackle. The soft, webby feathers from the neck of a domestic hen have just the right texture. Small body feathers from game-bird species are also effective, including those of partridge, grouse, snipe and woodcock. Other plumage is also used, such as that of the moorhen, but the use of dotterel, owl and plover, once traditional spider pattern materials, is now, fortunately, prohibited.

Although the March Brown bears the title of a real insect the combination of a hare's fur body, a brown partridge hackle and a wing of hen pheasant secondaries produces a pattern which will take fish in a wide range of water types and conditions and usually when there are no natural march browns!

The rocky, gravelly flow of rain-fed rivers is where spider patterns were developed. Their sparseness and economy of dressing fits in well with the feel of the river. Trout and grayling from these waters lack the rich, relaxed habitat of their chalkstream cousins. In the more broken water, their food is harder to come by, giving them a lean, sharper look. They are opportunistic, and a large part of their diet comes from terrestrial insects. However, small spider patterns, which can suggest a wide range of small creatures, are extremely effective: Snipe and Purple, Partridge and Orange, Waterhen Bloa and the intriguingly named Dark Watchet.

HACKLED WET FLIES

Similar in form to the spiders, simple hackled wet flies are usually a little more involved in their tying but still lack a wing. Among the most popular are the Pennell series, including the Black Pennell and the Claret Pennell, plus the Ke-He, Coch-y-bondhu and the Red Tag.

WINGED WET FLIES

The winged wet fly is the traditional profile, and still the most widely used. Tied in a variety of colours and materials, it may be used imitatively as a suggestion of a hatching or drowned aquatic insect, or in brighter garb as a general attractor.

In an imitative role are wet-fly patterns such as Greenwell's Glory, Blae and Black and Sooty Olive. Most are tied in muted colours, often with wings of grey mallard or starling primary feather. These shades

of grey nicely imitate the natural, smoky colours of an aquatic insect's wings. One prime example, the Greenwell's Glory, was designed back in the mid-nineteenth century to imitate the upwing flies on the River Tweed. It remains a deadly fly to this day.

At the other end of the scale, gaudier patterns such as the Dunkeld, Butcher, and Teal, Blue and Silver work as attractors, stimulating the trout to take out of aggression or general curiosity. Even these contain an element of imitation. Patterns with flashy silver or gold bodies overlaid with a darker, contrasting wing make a reasonable representation of a tiny fish.

Somewhere in the middle are the general deceivers; patterns which imitate nothing specific but which give a good impression of a small, living creature. A large proportion of the greatest of all winged wet flies fall into this category; patterns such as the Mallard and Claret, Connemara Black, Grouse and Claret, Hare's Ear, Cinnamon and Gold, the All-Rounder – the list goes on.

As in more imitative wet flies, wings of mallard and starling primary feather figure in many patterns. However, other more mottled feathers, such as bronze mallard, teal flank, grouse wing, hen pheasant tail and their wing secondaries are widely used. These plumages give a wonderful texture to any fly, suggesting anything from a caddis-fly to a shrimp, from a midge to a small fish. More importantly, they produce a fly which looks edible.

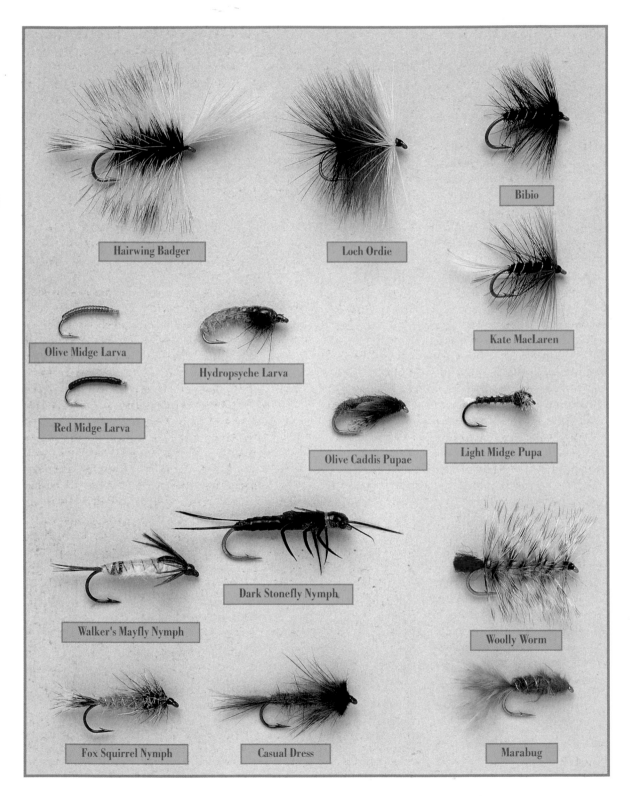

Hairwing Badger

Loch Ordie

Bibio

Kate MacLaren

Olive Midge Larva

Red Midge Larva

Hydropsyche Larva

Olive Caddis Pupae

Light Midge Pupa

Walker's Mayfly Nymph

Dark Stonefly Nymph

Woolly Worm

Fox Squirrel Nymph

Casual Dress

Marabug

PALMERED WET FLIES

The technique of palmering a hackle – winding it over the body of the fly – is one widely used in the tying of wet flies. It produces a dense, water-resistant profile which works superbly in the water, especially when pulled through a good wave. For this reason it is much used in loch and lake patterns.

Here the boat-fishing technique known as 'loch-style' is often used. This method can be deadly when conditions are warm and overcast and there is a good rolling wave. In such circumstances trout will often fall for a palmered fly fished on the top dropper and 'bobbed' through the top of the wave. What seems to attract them is the disturbance the fly makes on the surface, and when they are really 'on', fish may roll on the fly right by the boat, taking in a really confident manner. Patterns such as Soldier Palmer, Wingless Wickham's, Old Nick, Flue Brush and Doobry are all successful with this method.

Big, windswept lakes are where palmered wet flies are at their best. Because of this, many have been developed for fishing on the lochs and loughs of Scotland and Ireland. Patterns such as Kate MacLaren, Bibio, Zulu and Loch Ordie all have a rich history, taking countless wild brown trout as well as sea-trout and salmon. They may be tied in a range of sizes from as small as 14, or even 16, up to a monstrous size 6 for when the wind really does blow. The average is a more sensible size 10 or 12.

The density of the hackle also makes a difference. The closer the turns of hackle, the denser the fly. For a fly to be used in light winds, the hackle may be reduced to four or five turns. Conversely, six to eight turns are better for a good wave, while ten or more closely butted turns are perfect for half a gale. These densely hackled patterns also work well for a technique known as dapping; a cross between wet-fly and dry-fly fishing. Here a large, bushy fly is not cast, but, by using a long rod and an ultra-light polypropylene line, is skipped over the wave-tops on the breeze. It is a deadly method on many big lakes, especially during Mayfly time and when daddy-long-legs are on the water.

Most normal palmered flies may be beefed-up for dapping. Two particular favourites are Kate MacLaren and Loch Ordie, the latter consisting entirely of various coloured hackles. Equally effective dapping flies may be produced by tightly winding a series of furnace or grizzle hackles along a size 6 or 8 wet-fly hook. For a really big wave, a forward-pointing wing of dyed squirrel tail gives extra visibility.

NYMPHS AND BUGS

47

Most nymph and bug patterns are designed, like wet flies, to fish sub-surface; unlike wet flies, they are normally intended to imitate a specific type of aquatic invertebrate.

Although the term 'nymph' describes a specific stage in some insects' lives, in fly-fishing it is used more generally to denote patterns which suggest insect larvae and pupae along with genuine nymphs, and even patterns which imitate crustaceans are often wrongly called nymphs. In discussing the various patterns, it pays to be more specific. So the various types of 'nymph' can be broken down into three main stages: larvae, pupae and the true nymphs.

Larvae patterns are tied to imitate creatures such as the bloodworm, the larval stage of the chironomid midge, alder-fly larvae and the various types of caddis grub, with or without cases. The fly's form reflects the insect which is being mimicked. Midge larvae are

Some aquatic insect groups such as the ephemeropterans and the damsel and dragonflies have a life cycle with an incomplete metamorphosis. This means that instead of the larvae–pupae–adult of the midge where each stage is very different from each other, there is just one aquatic stage, the nymph. Typically nymphs are very similar in shape to the adults, usually being smaller until fully mature, and lacking wings.

small, worm-like creatures in red, green and brown, and imitations are little more than silk wound on the hook-shank. Caddis larvae imitations are usually much bigger and, in their cased form, much thicker and heavier and designed to fish along the river or lake bottom.

Pupae are the next stage, and as far as aquatic insects are concerned, artificials are tied to imitate midge and caddis pupae, though, like their larvae, they are quite different in size and shape. Pupae of the midge are tied with a slim, slightly tapering abdomen with a bulbous thorax, usually tipped with white filaments suggesting the breathers of the natural. Caddis pupae, on the other hand, are more robust, with a plump abdomen and a less pronounced thorax. However, the legs and wing-cases are much more visible, as are the trailing antennae.

True artificial nymphs are patterns tied to represent a vast wealth of aquatic creatures from the nymphs of ephemerids and stoneflies to those of dragonflies and damselflies. Although specific differences exist between patterns imitating the various creatures, nymph patterns all have a basic design. They usually have tails, the abdomen is tied quite slim, and the thorax is more pronounced and bulbous. Around the thorax the legs are imitated by a hackle, and the pattern is usually completed with wing-cases, suggesting the often noticeable immature wings trapped within the nymph's skin.

Jim Teeny of Portland, Oregon, is a great fly-fisher with a simple philosophy when it comes to tying flies. His Teeny Nymph, with its body and legs of either natural or dyed cock pheasant tail is an impressionistic pattern imitating nothing in particular, simply something alive and, to the trout, potentially edible. It may be tied in a wide range of sizes and colours.

The question of what is and isn't a nymph is clouded by the many more impressionistic patterns intended to imitate not a specific stage or species, but to suggest something alive and edible to the trout. Patterns such as the Hare's-ear Nymph, the Pheasant Tail Nymph, the Teeny Nymph and the Fox Squirrel Nymph work superbly in a variety of situations, particularly when the fish are looking for a meal but targeting nothing special. Many of these patterns, depending on size or how thick the body is, can represent anything from a tiny ephemerid nymph to a hulking great caddis larva.

The term 'bug' is usually used to denote a pattern which suggests a non-specific creature. Otherwise it is used for imitations of crustaceans such as the freshwater shrimp, *Gammarus*, or the hog-louse, *Asellus*. Most are chunky and often heavily weighted to fish along the bottom where the naturals are found. A number of shrimp and hog-louse imitations are tied, especially the former, but less specific patterns also take many fish in both rivers and stillwaters. Patterns which fall into this latter category include the Woolly Worm, Lead Bug, Four-water Favourite, Goldhead Bug, The Monty and the Grayling Bug.

LURES

Whether these weird and wonderful creations are called lures or bucktails and streamers depends on which side of the Atlantic you are on. The American terms of bucktails and streamers are probably more descriptive than our own, and less likely to make an onlooker think a spinner or plug is being used. But ask any reservoir angler what pattern of streamer he is using and he will look at you as if you have two heads!

Lures may be broken down into two main groups: hairwings or bucktails; and featherwings or streamers. Both terms amply describe the wing material of each type. In the hairwing it can be anything from bucktail to squirrel, calf-tail, badger, goat, rabbit, or even bear hair. Bucktail, that is the hair taken from the tail of an American white-tailed deer, is probably the most widely used; it is readily available, may be dyed a wide number of colours and, being up to 3–4in long, can be used for patterns of widely differing size.

Squirrel is also used a great deal, especially now that the process of bleaching and dying has been well

The Matuka style of winging hails from New Zealand. It is a technique which has become popular around the world for winging streamer patterns. Many different materials may be used such as cock and hen pheasant and partridge body hackles plus cock and hen hackles. Its main advantage is that by tying the wing securely to the top of the body the wing will not flip under the hook bend during casting.

developed. Whereas a wing of dyed grey squirrel was always rather dark, caused by the natural colour of the hair showing through, bleaching the tail first enables wonderfully bright and vibrant colours to be achieved. Being relatively soft and malleable, squirrel is a perfect material for winging smaller patterns, from a size 6 longshank down to a size 10 or 12 wet-fly hook. Many popular stillwater lures use it, including The Goldie, Sweeny Todd, Church Fry and Whisky Fly.

Rabbit fur has also become increasingly popular for hairwings although, being rather short in the fibre, and soft and mobile, it works best on mini-lure patterns tied on size 10 or 12 hooks. The main exception is the Zonker series, a range of flies which use rabbit not in tufts, but still on the skin. The skin is cut into thin strips, laid along the top of the hook, and secured to it either at the tail end or by having a wire rib wound through it in what is known as Matuka style. This allows very large patterns to be tied, either as general attractors or to imitate small fish such as roach or bullheads. Mink, which is similar, but has a shorter hair, is also an effective material, if sometimes difficult to obtain. It forms the base of one of the most deadly stillwater fry imitations of all – The Minkie. With its sensuous wiggle, produced by a tail of mink strip, the pattern has taken many big reservoir browns and rainbows.

Artificial hairs are also becoming more widely used, not simply the fine tinsel strands, such as Flashabou and Crystal Hair, which can be used either instead of or to add sparkle to an ordinary wing, but hair substitutes. Products such as Fishair, Polywiggle SLF and lately Ghost Fiber are all useful for streamer wings.

The technique of using materials such as gold, silver and copper Flashabou for the entire wing of large, reservoir lures has created a range of patterns which have taken more than their fair share of specimen rainbows and browns. The overall effect is somewhat like a Christmas tree decoration, which is not surprising in view of the source of some of the materials. However, though the lure may look an abomination in the hand, in the water, the soft tinsel strands pulse and sparkle beautifully. Tied either as tube-flies or as tandems, with two longshank hooks, these enormous Christmas tree lures certainly attract the bigger fish.

It would be remiss not to mention the Muddler. Originated by the American Don Gapen as an imitation of a small fish, it has spawned a vast number of patterns, deadly for species as varied as sailfish and tuna, salmon and trout. Indeed, it would be difficult to think of a single gamefish species, freshwater or salt, which hasn't succumbed to the allure of the Muddler.

Although Muddlers may be tied with hairwings or featherwings, their basic component is deerhair, so they are more hair than feather. The technique of producing a Muddler involves spinning deerhair on to the shank of the hook, usually just behind the eye. Because

Not all Muddlers have to be large streamers or fish imitations. The browns and dun shades of natural deer body hair lend themselves beautifully to imitating caddis flies or hoppers. Tied in small sizes, Muddlers, such as this Grenadier Muddler, also give added attraction to many standard wet-fly patterns.

Olive Zonker

Gilled zonker

Black Chenille

Whisky Fly

Thunder Creek

Spruce

Appetizer

Dahlberg Diver

SLF Mickey Finn

Original Muddler

Pulsar Tandem

Black Ghost. This handsome American streamer is a general pattern though it makes a passable impression of a small coarse fish. It uses two pairs of white cock neck or saddle hackles tied back to back to form the wing which can be tied up to twice the length of the body to impart maximum action.

the individual hairs are hollow and easily compressed, they flare when a thread is pulled tightly into them.

Flaring the hair and allowing it to spin around the hook-shank forms a compressed and buoyant head which can be trimmed with scissors to the profile required. This can range from a tight, teardrop form to a larger, more bulbous shape which can be 'popped' along the surface, making one hell of a disturbance. Another popular method is the Dahlberg style, devised by Larry Dahlberg of Minnesota, USA. Forming a large, upright collar to the upper trailing edge and sides of the Muddler head, and then stiffening it with fly-tying varnish, makes the pattern dip and dive as it is retrieved. Dahlberg's Diver makes a superb fry pattern.

Deerhair can also be used to produce entire flies. The very effective Floating Fry, or Spondoolie, is a prime example. It is constructed by spinning white deerhair the entire length of a size 4 or 2 longshank hook. The resulting mess is then trimmed into the shape of a small fish, being left either plain white or coloured with waterproof marker pens. The resulting imitation is deadly. Because the combination of deerhair and hook is only just buoyant enough to float, the Spondoolie sits right in the surface film. The pattern is usually tied so that it floats on its side, in the same manner as a small dying fish.

Streamers or featherwings, as their name implies, have wings constructed from feathers, anything from domestic chicken hackles, gamebird body feathers, such as those of the ring-necked pheasant, or duck flank feathers to the soft and highly mobile marabou.

Feather wings or streamers originally had wings of domestic chicken feathers taken either from the neck or cape of the bird. These hackles were cheap and easy to obtain and came in a wide range of natural colours, while the lighter shades, such as white and cream, could be dyed a variety of colours. The hackles are usually used as one or two pairs placed back to back, so that the natural curves of the feathers cancel one another out, producing a perfectly straight wing. This style of wing is still used widely in patterns such as Black Ghost, Spruce, White Lure and Black Chenille.

Many featherwinged lures are tied to represent small fish. Trout are predatory, and at certain times of year, especially during late summer and early autumn, they become committed fish-eaters. To catch them you often have to resort to an 'imitative' lure. If that sounds a contradiction, then think again. Trout can become preoccupied when fry-feeding and will fall most readily to a pattern which has the basic size and shape of a small fish. When they are feeding on fry 3–4in long, a lure the same size is needed. To achieve this, and still have something which is castable on a fly-rod, two normal hooks may be rigged in tandem, a double lure being tied on this set-up. The hook may be joined either by thick nylon monofilament or braided mono of about 30lb breaking-strain. Wire should be avoided, as it may eventually fatigue and break.

Hackles from domestic fowl may also be used in the Matuka-style lure. This employs a method developed in New Zealand where the feather used came from the matuka bird. Today, easier-to-obtain feathers are used, such as cock and hen hackles, and hen pheasant body-feathers. In each case the hackles are placed back to back in the usual manner and tied in at the head. They are then secured to the top of the lure's body with turns of ribbing material. The effect is much like a fish's dorsal fin and has the advantage that it never flips round to become caught under the bend of the hook during casting. This ensures that a Matuka-style fly always fishes on an even keel.

Effective Matuka patterns include Ace of Spades, Badger Matuka and Olive Matuka.

MARABOU STREAMERS

It is difficult to know where to start with marabou-tied streamers, such has been their impact on trout fishing. Marabou originally came from the marabou stork, but today the material is obtained from the white domestic turkey, which must be a great relief to the stork!

51

Turkey marabou is a quite superb material for winging streamers and adding tails to weighted patterns such as Tadpoles. When wet, the soft fluffy marabou pulses seductively in the water producing an action which trout find hard to resist. This action can be improved by using a tail as much as three inches long. Rather than nipping at the long tail the fish simply sucks the whole thing down.

nymph, a leech or even a small fish such as a bullhead or sculpin.

Marabou is also used in the dressing of the Booby, a pattern which has perhaps caused more controversy on the stillwater trout scene than any other. Like the Tadpole, the Booby takes its action from a long tail of dyed marabou, but unlike the fly with a weighted head, the Booby is buoyant. The buoyancy is achieved by using closed-cell foam, such as Ethafoam, to create two large, bulbous eyes, and to make the Booby fish close to the bottom, it is connected to an ultra-fast sinking fly-line and a short leader. The action, though similar to that of the Tadpole, works in reverse, with the Booby rising on a pause in the retrieve rather than sinking. A related pattern, the Rassler, has a body made entirely from Ethafoam. This makes it extremely buoyant and especially effective as a fry imitation to be fished deep around submerged weed beds.

This soft, mobile feather has been incorporated into a vast range of patterns, where its wonderfully sinuous action has lead to the downfall of thousands of trout.

Marabou comes alive in the water. The softness of the feather makes it extremely responsive, allowing it to twitch and pulse with every move of the retrieve, a motion which may be varied by altering the rate of retrieve or by moving the rod-top. In clear water, a trout may be seen to swim several yards across a pool to nail a marabou-tailed fly, especially if it is given an extra seductive wiggle at the end of the retrieve.

Many modern streamer patterns have marabou somewhere in their design, as a wing, a tail, or sometimes both. Patterns such as Dog Nobblers, Tadpoles, Tinheads and Woolly Buggers, in all their various colour combinations, take fish in rivers as well as lakes and reservoirs. Like other types of lure, they may be tied in bright garish hues, stimulating the fish to take out of aggression or curiosity. However, the use of marabou as a tail in conjunction with a weighted head produces a superb, wiggling action. This lends itself perfectly to patterns tied in more sombre, natural colours to suggest a living creature such as a damselfly

As a bottom grubbing pattern there is little to beat a Woolly Bugger. The combination of a mobile marabou tail and a palmered hackle produce a real mouthful which big fish particularly find to their liking. It may be tied in a wide range of colours though usually in natural hues such as brown, olive and black.

3 FLY CASTING

Most fly-fishermen are self-taught and a walk around any stillwater fishery will reveal many and varied casting techniques, some of them not pretty to watch. But we all have to start somewhere, and once a newcomer has managed to put out most of a standard fly-line in a fairly straight line, he probably feels that is far enough for him to catch as many trout as he wants.

Bad casting habits can be put right by a professional instructor, but it is better to have proper casting tuition from the very beginning. Instruction is not expensive, and a good video on the subject of casting will help far more than the written word alone.

Beginners obtain casting proficiency surprisingly quickly with a good instructor, especially when he has only a small group of pupils. Once the major obstacles are mastered – such as stance, grip, timing, left-hand movement (if right-handed) and delivery – progress can be remarkable, extending into techniques more specialized than the simple overhead cast.

Fly-casting can become an obsession, and for dedicated tournament casters catching trout becomes a secondary matter. But some, such as Hywel Morgan, of Wales, manage both very well. Reservoir anglers often have unwitting casting competitions with their neighbour, rather than thinking properly about what their flies are doing. But most anglers, once they can cast reasonably well, tend to concentrate solely on catching trout.

Balanced tackle is important, and a good outfit is a middle-to-tip-actioned carbon fly-rod of 9½–10ft matched with a weight-forward AFTM 7 or 8 fly-line. With the line extended, a normal fishing situation sees the line retrieved, a little roll-cast made to lift the line off or out of the water and into the air, and two speedy false-casts to build up line speed, with the double-haul employed if extra shooting distance is wanted.

Whereas a full fly-line is about 30yd long, a shooting-head is from 10–12yd. The latter, attached to fine nylon backing, is the ultimate for distance-casting, and its use can soon be mastered once a full fly-line can be handled well. Distances of 40yd are normal for most shooting-head fishers, giving advantage on big stillwaters.

Casting cannot be learned properly from the written word, but reading about it does put you in the right frame of mind, and studying a picture sequence of the various movements can help a lot. Then it is a question of practise, practise, practise.

1 The correct grip of the cork fly-rod handle and a proper stance are all important. The thumb should be on top of the rod reaching towards the top of the cork, and a right-hander should stand with his left foot forward to achieve good balance.

2 An accomplished caster is not too bothered about which way the wind is blowing, but a beginner prefers to

Reservoir trout move well out from the bank during the day in early summer. This fly-fisher has found fish nymph-feeding in shallow water and has decided to wade out to try for them.

54

LEFT Deep-water wading is not necessary in early-season reservoir fishing. Here a roll-cast is about to be made with the rod-and-line position spot on. The roll-cast is used here as a preliminary to lift the fly-line from the water before going into the overhead back-cast.

BELOW The roll-cast develops. The rod is brought sharply forward while the left hand pulls back line before releasing it.

BOTTOM After two overhead false casts, when plenty of line is let out, the whole fly-line shoots through the rings to give 30m between rod and flies.

have the wind at his back. Given a speedy penetration of line into the back-cast, it is possible, with good timing and a tight loop, to cast much further than if the air were still.

3 The roll-cast is important because it is used a lot in river fishing where overgrown trees make overhead casting out of the question. It also forms the first component of a long single- or double-haul cast.

Lift the rod and bring the line back slowly over the water; then move the rod back behind the body. Stop the movement briefly while the surface tension clings to the floating line. Then bring the rod forward fast and stop with the tip at shoulder height. Always try to practice on water rather than grass.

4 To make the single-haul over-head cast, begin with a normal short roll-cast to straighten the line. As it straightens, lift the rod firmly while hauling downwards on the line with the left hand. This accelerates the line-speed and fully loads the rod ready for the forward cast. As the forward cast reaches the point of delivery, give a short mini-haul to put 'zip' into the distance of the cast.

Control the line while it is shooting forward by allowing it to travel through an extra 'ring' formed by the index finger and thumb. For a perfect straight-line delivery, pinch the line just before it hits the water. Everything then straightens – fly-line, nylon leader and fly.

A perfect shot of the long haul needed before the final line-shoot to give the extra acceleration of line speed needed to cast long distances.

5 Double-haul casting is a natural progression for any fly-fisher. Mastery of it makes it easier to attain much greater distances, and to catch more fish. The double-haul is exactly as it sounds, with the hauls made at exactly the same time as the rod is punched on the back and forward casts. The hauls should be short and fast. Practising false casting with about 10 metres of line aerialized helps to establish the feel of when things are coming right. It's rather like learning to swim or to ride a bike: once it is mastered, you have the skill for life.

This fly-fisher has selected a good bank position. The slight sideways breeze allows the fly-line to drift the flies round naturally.

6 Most fly-fishermen avoid casting into the wind, yet that is often
what is needed to achieve a good
catch. The greatest problem is that
the nylon leader is blown back
once the line begins to straighten
and finishes in a tangle, making it
useless. One remedy is to use a
shorter leader, as presentation is
not so important in rough water.
Another is to shoot the line low,
cutting it under the wind, and to
use the fly-line pinch method to
turn the cast over.

7 A style known as the steeple-
cast is useful when an overhead
cast is difficult because of a dam
wall or high bushes behind. The
line is thrown high on the back-
cast and stopped short before
being delivered in a low, acceler-
ated forward cast. Fishing off a
dam wall demands a regular check
of hook-points; a hook has only to
clip the stonework to bend or
break a point.

8 Casting with the wind blowing
strongly on to his right side can be

TOP Trees and overhanging branches can be a problem on small fisheries. Charles Jardine takes advantage of a clear area to extend some line, with slack line
ready to be shot.

MIDDLE Into the back-cast: the line straightens and
compresses the rod, and the forward cast begins.

LEFT A snappy forward cast, and out it all goes.

dangerous for a right-handed caster, with a high risk of hooking himself on a normal overhead cast. Some fly-fishers turn to face inland, their backs to the water, and deliver a back-handed cast. This can be effective in well-practised hands, and eliminates the danger of hooking oneself on the forward cast.

Given a clear back-cast area, a cast in which the rod is worked horizontally with the same hauling method as in the overhead cast can be effective. It, too, keeps the fly well away from the fisherman's body on the forward shoot.

9 Wet-fly fishing from a drifting boat entails using a soft, longish rod of about 11ft. The length is not to enhance casting, but to enable the angler to dibble the top dropper well away from the boat. The soft action is needed to withstand a close-range hard take on light nylon, the length giving a cushioning effect. Casts should be short and repetitive as the boat drifts downwind. The technique has been described as 'stroking the water'.

10 River or stream fishing often demands short but perfect casts with a lightweight rod of 8ft or less and a

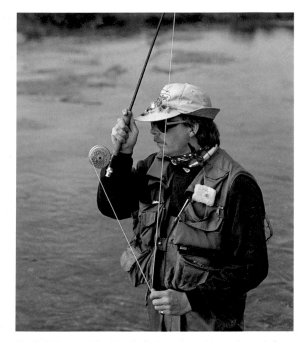

River fly-fishing, especially with a dry fly, demands precision casting, and often a short cast to land the fly a foot or so upstream of a rise-form.

Long-range casting is sometimes needed on big, wide rivers, and then a sink-tip line can be helpful. Here the angler is trying to reach the deep central pool.

ABOVE A shallow, tumbling stream typifies the situation in which short, accurate casts are needed. Casting must be upstream so the fish also facing upstream can be approached from behind.

RIGHT In crystal-clear water and bright conditions it pays to keep a low profile by kneeling on the bank before making as delicate a cast as possible.

size 4 floating fly-line. A tapered hollow-braided leader with only a short (3ft) length of tippet nylon provides perfect turnover for dry-fly fishing.

Given a fish rising regularly at the same spot, the fly really needs to land a foot or two upstream of the rise,

leaving the current to do the rest. False casting should enable just enough fly-line to be extended to the exact length. Over-casting frightens a trout; under-casting means that it doesn't see the fly.

4 LURE FISHING

Lure fishing, or streamer fishing, is a major trout-catching technique the world over. In the old purist days in Britain any large fly or lure pattern was looked upon as an invention of the devil. Early patterns had names such as Demon or Terror, but soon small fish-imitating patterns began to be used, and some, such as Tom Ivens' Jersy Herd and Dick Shrive's Missionary are still used.

Lure fishing became popular in the early 1960s because it often accounted for the largest trout. Dick Walker was then active in stillwater fishing, and it was he who created two lures intended for use at Grafham, the Polystickle and the Sweeney Todd. It was soon found that these patterns worked well almost anywhere. At about the same time the Church Fry (Bob Church) was designed to imitate the small perch in Ravensthorpe and Pitsford reservoirs. Then came the deadly Black Chenille and the Appetiser. These two lures were the first British patterns to employ chenille and marabou in their dressings. The Appetiser is still regarded as one of the best small fish-imitators and catcher of large trout.

Early-season lure fishing at reservoirs can be productive, especially to black-based small lures. Dress sensibly to beat the wind, wet and cold, because no protection from the elements can be found on an exposed bank.

One of the first British patterns to use chenille in its dressing, the Church Fry has been taking reservoir trout since the sixties.

Another pattern that caused a stir was Don Gapen's Muddler Minnow from America. This, too, has stood the test of time and now has many variants. The next breakthrough came in about 1980 when Trevor Housby, from Hampshire, introduced us to the infamous Dog Nobbler. This lure had an enticing action which trout everywhere seemed unable to resist. But why did Trevor give it such a name? He reckoned it sorted out the big old 'dog' trout when other lures or flies failed, and he wasn't far wrong!

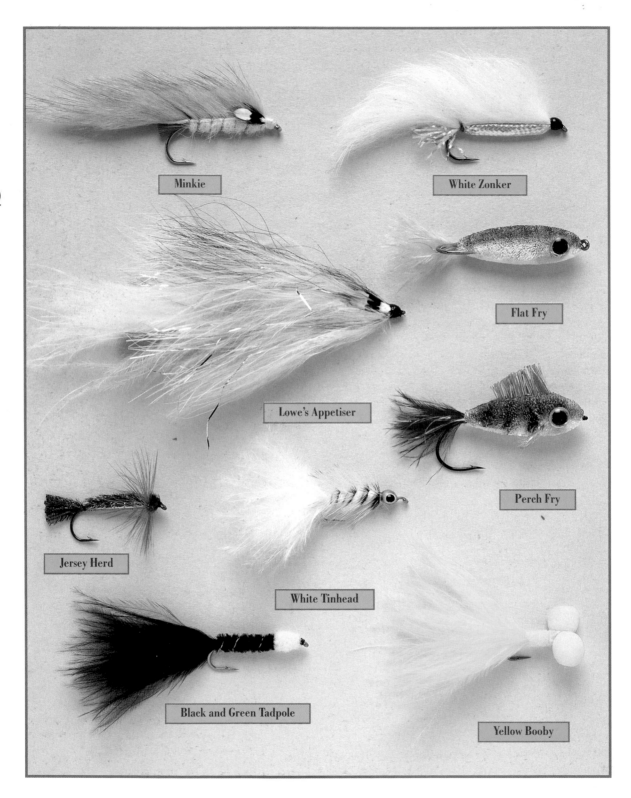

Minkie

White Zonker

Flat Fry

Lowe's Appetiser

Perch Fry

Jersey Herd

White Tinhead

Black and Green Tadpole

Yellow Booby

Other lure designs followed. The Zonker, which incorporates a strip of rabbit skin, is popular, and so are the Boobies, rather like buoyant versions of the Dog Nobbler. Then we have the deadly Tinheads, which have a soldered blob for a head which is either painted with eyes or is a plain colour, including fluorescent. Goldhead lures, which, initially were river nymph patterns, have a gold-plated brass ball around the hook to form the head. To these can be added a whole new series of floating-fry patterns which are fished on a floating line on the surface or on a fast-sinking line with a short leader, when the lure floats off the bottom.

Early-season trout fishing is ideal for the use of small lures. With the trout's common food still hibernating or buried in the bottom silt as larvae, the fish don't have a lot of choice. As water temperatures are still low, the trout feed much less frequently than they do in early to mid-summer. At this time a black-based mini-lure fished slowly along the weedless bottom gives a reasonable chance of hooking a trout. If a floating, sink-tip or intermediate fly-line is preferred, then a weighted Black Tadpole on a size 10 or 8 hook is a good choice.

To be really successful at this time of year demands a rather special approach. Set up with a powerful rod, a fly-reel with a specially built-up spindle, 100 metres of flat black nylon backing, and a size 9 or 10 medium-sinking shooting-head of about 12yd. Carry no more kit in your pockets than is essential, i.e. nylon, flies and priest. Then cast long distances and fish along the

ABOVE A Black Tadpole stripped quickly across the top at dusk regularly produces the heaviest trout of the day at many reservoirs.

Striving for distance. This fly-fisher, lure fishing from the bank, is in a favourable crosswind position, with the wind left to right. Fish will almost certainly be within his casting distance in such ideal conditions.

bottom, making only a few casts in each spot before moving on. With the sinking fly-line weighted lures will be unnecessary, so try an ordinary Black Tadpole or Viva, or even one of the old favourites, Black Chenille or Ace of Spades, tied on longshank 10 or 8 hooks. A lot of ground can be covered fishing thus on a reservoir, and the permitted eight-fish limit is often achieved.

Those who choose to fish deep water off a dam wall early in the season have seen a specialized approach evolve. The method, known as Booby fishing, uses a fast-sinking shooting-head fished on an outfit similar to that described, but with a leader of only 2ft instead of 13ft. This short leader allows the Booby to float up from the bottom to the same distance as the length of nylon, and a series of jerky twitches gives it an irresistible rise-and-fall action. Many takes come when the Booby is static, which is frowned upon by fly-fishers and which has caused the lure to be banned at some small fisheries. One thing is sure: the technique has accounted for a number of double-figure rainbows

The Viva uses the black and fluorescent green combination which crops up in many modern stillwater trout patterns. It is a deadly fly from the first cast of the season to the last.

and browns at reservoirs such as Grafham, which is known for its big grown-on trout.

A powerful rod, a high-D fast-sink shooting-head on a wide-diameter Lineshooter reel, a good-quality nylon leader and a selection of various Booby lures is a good choice of tackle with which to fish from a dam wall or in a concrete-bowl type of reservoir.

Before describing floating-fry fly-fishing, it is perhaps best to explain how a pattern is 'tied', because it is model-making rather than fly-tying!

The materials needed are size 6 longshank hooks, some flat white Ethafoam (the kind that fly-boxes are lined with is ideal) and some pearl Mylar piping. Cut some shapes out of the Ethafoam to represent the back and tail of the lure. Cut a length of pearl Mylar a little longer than the hookshank, slide it along the shank and secure it at both the bend and the eye with white tying silk. Allow the tail-end to fray a little. Now tie in the V-tail end of Ethafoam at the hook-bend and the straight end at the eye. Build up a well-shaped head and varnish, painting on eyes, which do seem to make the lure more effective.

RIGHT Jeremy Herrmann with a fine brace of grown-on rainbows from Farmoor Reservoir, Oxfordshire. Here he fishes the Booby method, holding the rod-tip slightly to the side so that takes can be seen and hit more easily.

BELOW Booby fishing is frowned upon by some, but in the right hands it is deadly.

The fishing method is simple. Locate shoals of fry around weed-beds or a boat jetty and almost certainly a few big trout will be about. But take note: fry-feeding trout feed well for half-an-hour or less and then rest for several hours before repeating the process. Patience is needed!

Do more fish-watching than fishing and observe where the pike-like attacks come as fry of roach or perch leap from the water in terror. The trout's fast lunge often stuns a few fry which then float to the surface, where they lie static or feebly flapping. Cast the floating fry into the area on a floating line and wait. Sooner or later, as the breeze drifts the lure along, the water will explode as a fish takes.

Other types of floating-fry patterns are ingenious. One is a Plastazote 'sideways' pattern developed with success at Rutland; another is the incredibly realistic Perch Fry tied with deerhair and coloured with a Pantone pen. Patterns such as these are best kept in a separate fly-box for use at that special time of year, late August until the end of October.

What if trout are fry-feeding, but will not look at floating-fry patterns? Try the Appetiser! It has accounted for many fry-feeding trout at most big reservoirs, in particular Henry Lowe's double-figure rainbow caught on a size 6 Appetiser from the seat on the Sludge Lagoon back at Grafham, and a 31lb 7oz limit for Bob Church in Savage's Creek, also at Grafham. The stories are endless! So if the floating-fry isn't working, change down to an intermediate fly-line and fish an Appetiser slowly through the fry-feeding area.

Trout begin to show signs of fry-feeding at the end of August, as their stomach contents prove.

David Barker, from Cambridge, and a Grafham regular, used a Minkie developed for Grafham fry-feeding trout to catch this magnificent grown-on rainbow of 13lb 13oz, an ultimate reservoir prize.

The American Zonker originally had a natural rabbit fur matuka-style tail and wing, and it soon built up a reputation for itself in this country. But the experts had to change it, and variations soon appeared. White with silver or pearl bodies became popular, but at Grafham the Minkie Zonker became the 'in' lure from

RIGHT A series of short, sharp twitches during the retrieve makes a lure with a marabou tail or wing pulsate, giving it more life and encouraging a trout to take.

BELOW Casting into the wind and lure-stripping with a floating line is a good summer tactic when the daphnia blooms are present. Jeremy Herrmann is playing a fast-moving rainbow merely by stripping or giving line, enabling him to keep in contact with the fish.

This rainbow took a Viva Booby lure on a 2ft leader and Hi-D fast-sink line.

FACTFILE

Lure fishing is not just a chuck-and-chance-it method as some would have us believe. It is a skilful way of fishing, as Jeremy Herrmann, the young and successful competition fisher, has proved in recent years. A good fly-fisher learns all methods and uses each at the appropriate time.

Fast-action rods are usually the best option for long-distance casting with shooting-heads. Specialized reels, such as the Lineshooter and Loop models, have built-up central spools to help prevent tangles with nylon backing.

Shooting-heads give a great advantage in terms of distance, which makes all the difference if fish are well out from the bank, as is always likely on popular fisheries. Invest in a shooting-head outfit if you intend to do much lure fishing. And remember, lure fishing can be every bit as imitative as fishing a nymph or dry fly.

the bank. At Grafham a long-tailed Minkie did the trick for Dave Barker when he fished from the boat jetty and broke the English wild rainbow trout record with a superb fish of 13lb 13oz.

When a reservoir becomes murky in rough weather, or when an algae bloom cuts the visibility to no more than a foot or so, colourful lures come into their own. A trout cannot take a lure if it cannot see it, and the strong fluorescent colours which show up best in these conditions will certainly take a few fish when all else fails. Use a slow figure-of-eight retrieve, as in nymph fishing. A fast-moving lure will soon be lost to the trout's sight.

5 WET-FLY FISHING

Wet-fly fishing is a term long used to describe the traditional method of using short-casting floating-line tactics from a drifting boat. It is also a river method used on rough streams where trout are plentiful and not too fussy.

But wet-fly fishing with many of the beautiful traditional fly patterns is no more than a memory for modern-day boat-drifters. Methods developed over the last 20 years simply produce more trout than ever before.

Loch-style fishing to International rules has been the starting point for many new tactics. Competitors who have regularly won major events have passed on their knowl-

Tal-y-Llyn, a jewel of West Wales. Set in magnificent scenery, it is a shallow, productive lake of 222 acres. Wild browns, supplemented with stocked browns, give good wet-fly sport, with always a chance of a sea-trout or salmon at the right time of year.

edge, resulting in a rise in standards even for only average performers.

Stocking policies on the big reservoirs of England and Wales, and now even on some Scottish lochs, have concentrated on rainbow trout rather than browns, usually around a 90 per cent/10 per cent split – and most anglers generally fish for the dominant species. Rainbows are more aggressive than browns, so mini-lure attractor patterns are successful, especially early and late in the season. At those times, fast-sinking fly-lines are used to great effect, but from June to September the floating line, with fast retrieves and bright flies also trigger the rainbows' natural aggression.

A wild Scottish brown trout, a perfect sporting fish. This one fell to a wet fly which was fished on one of the Thurso lochs in Caithness.

Hot Spot Wickham's

Old Nick

Jungle Cock Viva

Mini Standard Muddler

Orange Mini Muddler

Orange Soldier Palmer

Pearl Invicta

Dunkeld

Loch Hope is a beautiful wild Scottish loch in the Highlands of Sutherland. Its wild brown trout are good to catch, but its sea-trout and salmon form the cream of the sport.

But it's not always like that. On some days a more imitative fly works best, and on any wild brown trout lough in Ireland, rainbow flies are best left at home because they don't work.

Fishing for early season trout from an anchored boat is also effective, but certainly not as challenging as drifting. But conditions are still too cold for fish to rise readily, even though a few chironomids may be hatching, and any chance of a good catch must depend on the fast-sinking line technique with a team of size 10 mini-lures, coupled with the use of a drogue set from a central broadside position to make the boat drift as slowly as possible. A drift over water 12ft deep or less is ideal, and if the wind allows a drift parallel to the shoreline, so much the better as the depth will remain constant.

A wild Welsh brown trout which fell to a wet fly in Lake Vyrnwy in mid-Wales. It took a Bibio.

A size 10 double-hooked pattern helps keep a team of flies down. Favoured patterns are Viva (with jungle cock cheeks), Cat's Whisker and Orange Tadpole. In fact the whole team can be built on variations of the main colours of these three patterns. The leader should be 6ft of 6lb or 5lb nylon to the top dropper, then 5ft to the centre, and a further 5ft to the point.

Perfect conditions for wet-fly fishing, overcast with a good ripple. The gillie works the boat with the back oar along the windward shoreline, where trout tend always to congregate.

If the wind is too strong, creating a fast drift, the boat can be slowed by means of a drogue secured at the central rowlock position. Brian Lead-better shows how.

The method known as the 'hang', developed at Grafham by Bob Church, is now an accepted cold-water tactic. The flies are cast on a long line and allowed to sink to the bottom, being retrieved in long, slow pulls before the rod is lifted sharply. This accelerates the flies' ascent from the bottom, but a further pause then allows them to hang for up to 30 seconds. It's amazing how many trout which were merely curiously following the flies now take the suspended static fly. Sometimes the top dropper is taken, but often the deep-lying middle dropper is the chosen one. Bite indication comes from watching the curve in the fly-line from rod-tip to the surface. When it straightens, strike! On good days fish pull the rod-tip down and virtually hook themselves.

At times, usually during the transition to warmer temperatures around the end of May, nothing seems to work. A fast-sinker fails, and then a floater. Now is the time to try a sink-tip line, perhaps with a size 12 Soldier Palmer as a top dropper, a hackled Claret Hatching Midge in the centre, and a hackled Pheasant Tail on the point. These nymph patterns have been changed by use of two full circular turns of hackle feather and now have a wet-fly look. It is a well-proven combination which has scored on the major reservoirs. The retrieve should be quite slow.

July sees water temperatures soaring, but also days of wind and grey, rolling clouds. Now is the time to try

International fly-fisher Brian Leadbetter practises the deadly sinking-line 'hang' technique.

Perfect hooking, right in the scissors of the jaw.

the surface-stripped Muddler on a floating fly-line. Some fly-fishers always fish a standard Muddler on the point, but it has equal importance as a top dropper, especially if other good flies in the team back it up: Dunkeld with jungle cock eyes, Appetizer, Fiery Brown, Soldier Palmer, Grenadier or Solwick. With a drogue to slow the boat, a long line is cast downwind and the flies stripped back through the waves as fast as possible. Several fish may follow before one is hooked, but it is exciting stuff!

Fish sometimes follow the Muddler only to turn and take one of the other flies on the leader. Although the standard gold-bodied Muddler is still the best fish-catcher, other patterns have their day. A silver-bodied standard Muddler can be good, or a pure white version. In the hottest weather an Orange Muddler is lethal, and later on in summer a Black Muddler comes good.

A former England fly-fishing team captain, Jim Collins, favours a method of wet-fly fishing which has brought him much success. It could be described as nymph feeding, but with size 14 or 16 wet flies. He has great faith in his simple style. With a size 7 floating

Orange is widely recognized as a deadly summer colour. The Grenadier, though a traditional pattern, has a really modern feel, and is as effective today as ever.

line for the big waters and as light a leader as possible (around 4lb) Jim's favourite patterns are Wickham's Fancy, Greenwell's Glory, Harry Tom, Invicta, Silver Invicta and Dunkeld.

Jim's method is to slow his boat down with a maxi 5ft square drogue and then to cast slightly at an angle to the wind. He pauses for the flies to sink a little and then retrieves in figure-of-eight nymphing style. Many anglers are too impatient to fish this method correctly, and soon resort to faster retrieving, but the technique works only with that slow, continuous retrieve.

By mid-season, stock rainbows that have grown on are decent fish, and most reservoir trout put up a great fight. They lose many of their spots to become bars of silver, and having been living on a rich diet of chironomids, olives and sedges, they are used to taking at or close to the surface. Now traditional short-line loch-style tactics prove their worth – and give so much pleasure if things go right. A lightweight floating fly-line

Good wet-fly conditions at Rutland Water, Britain's largest man-made lake at 3,300 acres. The large, stable boats are ideal for drift fishing.

Well-known Bristol fly-fisher Les Toogood hooks a lively rainbow on wet fly at famous Blagdon Reservoir, set in the Mendip Hills.

BELOW Reservoir rainbows are bright, silver and muscle-packed during the summer, and their fighting abilities beat all others.

BELOW Wet-fly fishing can be successful from the bank in remote places such as this, but it is best practised from a drifting boat.

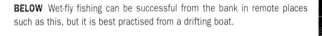

on a soft-actioned 11ft rod is a good set-up, but the method depends on the angler's ability to 'dibble' his top dropper, or 'bob' fly, with enticing delicacy. Two masters of this method are Brian Leadbetter and Terry Oliver. Both seem to have the knack of rising trout seemingly from nowhere.

The size of hackled body fly used depends on the height of the wave. For example, a light ripple indicates a size 14, in a 1ft wave a size 12 would do; and a size 10 for rougher water. Soldier Palmer variants, Wingless Wickham variants, Hoppers and Daddy-long-legs are all bushy patterns which create the disturbance that a dancing bob-fly needs to make.

A fish taken on a wet fly from the bank.

The Ginger Quill is a traditional winged wet fly. It uses stripped peacock eye quill to give a life-like segmented effect to the body. It is a great pattern during a hatch of brown midge.

In late summer, catching daphnia-feeding fish entails finding the depth at which the rainbows concentrate; near to the surface on dull, cloudy days, and deeper

Michael Dawnay uses a long, soft rod, traditional for wet-fly fishing, to bring a good Welsh brown to net.

FACTFILE

A full set of fly-lines is needed to be able to fish wet fly all season, including size 6 and size 8 weight-forward floaters. A very fast sink line, a sink-tip and an intermediate are also 'musts', all size 7 or 8 weight-forward. Rods should give a choice of powerful 10ft long-caster, a 10½ft all-rounder for multi-purpose use, and an 11ft rod for bob-fly fishing.

An extending boat seat which fits over the thwarts gives a high, comfortable casting position and a drogue is essential – but take a G-clamp with you to fit on the central gunwale. Remember, too, that a boat on a large reservoir offers no escape from either the wind or the rain. Have a full set of good waterproof clothing with you.

down during bright sunny weather. At such times hot orange really comes good. So find the depth and use an orange-based mini-lure such as Peach Doll, Old Nick or Orange Chenille and strip back quite fast.

The time comes when the trout become really preoccupied in feeding, and then they are very difficult to tempt. It is when newly hatched coarse fish pin-fry are about half-an-inch long and shoaling in their billions. Most flies are ignored, but the Silver Invicta, size 14, is a traditional pattern worth trying.

It is far better, however, to create one's own pin-fry patterns, using clear, stretched polythene over a silver and red thorax underbody, and building up a black head with the tying silk before painting on eyes. This type of fly seems to take a few fish when all else fails.

The retrieve for these methods can be at various speeds from slow to fast stripping, or by a slow figure-of-eight retrieve. The 'roly-poly' continuous hand-over-hand retrieve has become popular, too, giving the effect of a trolled fly. It can be deadly at times.

6 STILLWATER NYMPH FISHING

The whole premise of nymph fishing is to imitate a small, aquatic invertebrate which is part of the trout's diet. This type of fly takes two forms: it is either a direct imitation of a specific creature such as a midge pupa, caddis larva, shrimp, and so on, or merely suggestive of something small, vulnerable and edible which may tempt an opportunist feeder such as the trout. But to imitate a living creature entails more than simply tying a fly to look like it; it also entails fishing the fly in a manner similar in movement and range to that of the real thing, to make it appear alive and as natural as possible.

On lakes this is not always easy. First impressions can be misleading, for it may seem that without a river's vagaries of current and changing flow, presenting a fly

Gordon Frazer's Fourwater Favourite uses a tail of brown rabbit fur to give it a seductive wiggle. The Goldhead Fourwater has the addition of a gold bead to give the fly extra weight and sparkle.

Nymph fishing can be from either boat or bank. If a boat is used, anchor it so that it doesn't swing on the anchor rope. This may entail using two anchors, one at either end of the boat. Failure to eliminate swing will make controlling the nymphs and seeing delicate takes all the more difficult. Don't anchor in water that is too deep. For much of the year, fish will be feeding in 6–12ft of water, and that is where you should be casting from a boat anchored 20yd or so upwind of the mark. Disturbance should be kept to a minimum, with the anchor always lowered gently over the side, never thrown in.

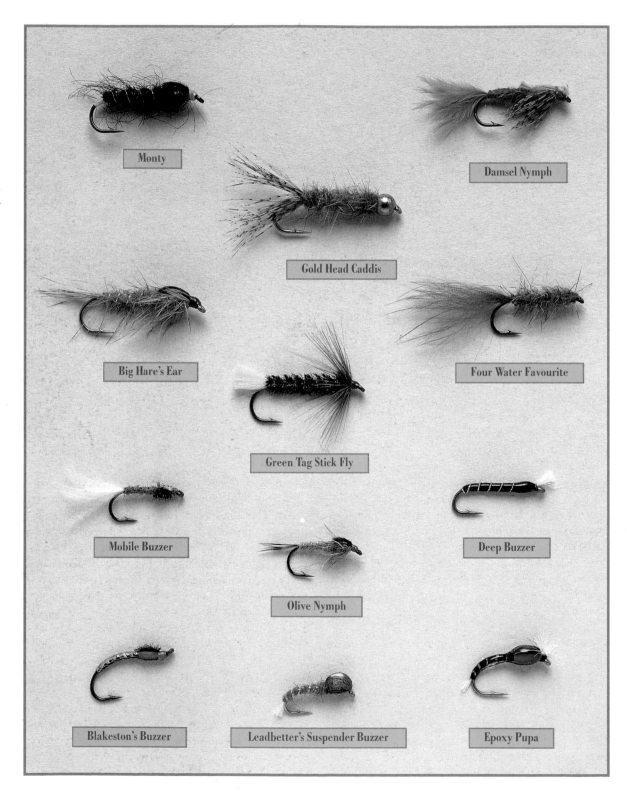

Monty

Damsel Nymph

Gold Head Caddis

Big Hare's Ear

Green Tag Stick Fly

Four Water Favourite

Mobile Buzzer

Olive Nymph

Deep Buzzer

Blakeston's Buzzer

Leadbetter's Suspender Buzzer

Epoxy Pupa

LEFT The Killer, with its neat simple profile, is a great point fly for general nymph fishing. It can be weighted, but usually relies on a heavy hook to help it sink.

BELOW The marrowspoon reveals that this brown trout had been feeding exclusively on the freshwater shrimp, *Gammarus*. Such feeding is common early in the season, when general aquatic insect activity is at a low ebb. Crustaceans, such as the shrimp and the hog-louse, are present in many waters throughout the season, and they are obvious targets when other food is short. A weighted Shrimp pattern fished slowly along the bottom is usually the most effective technique.

on stillwater is a simple matter. You don't have to fish for long to realize how wrong this assumption is. Wind and wave action, and the subsurface currents which they produce, are all problems for the stillwater nymph-fisher to solve if a fly is to be presented in a lifelike manner. Depth adds another dimension; you need to work out at what level the target is feeding and how to fish a small, imitative pattern at anything up to 20ft down.

While it is possible to fish a nymph on any density of fly line, floating and intermediate lines are the most useful. A floating line is the most versatile of all because, by using flies which sink at various rates, you are able to cover a wide range of water depths and feeding levels. You can also fish them slowly, without the constant danger of having them dragged into the bottom by a sinking line. This latter point is vitally important, for to fish nymphs successfully, you need to move them slowly.

There is always the exception. There are times when trout will pounce upon a quickly retrieved nymph to the exclusion of all else. But for the bulk of nymph fishing the aim is to fish the pattern slowly or even completely static, though in this instance 'static' is somewhat of a misnomer. Always remember that you are trying to suggest a small invertebrate, and here a little practical field work pays. Try to find a natural midge pupa, caddis larva or shrimp swimming in the margins. Watch how it moves; its action and speed.

The first thing you notice is that even real sprinters such as the shrimp move quite slowly in comparison with a normal wet-fly retrieve rate. Caddis larvae and midge pupae are almost stationary by comparison, taking minutes to move only a few inches. Midge pupae, because they are free-swimming are also strongly affected by water movement, and this is a major key in the effective fishing of midge pupae imitations. Although surface activity associated with trout taking emerging midge pupae is the more obvious, most pupae are taken well below the surface, where they reveal no obvious sign of feeding fish. This offers a real problem to the aspiring nymph-fisher. If you can't see what the fish are taking, how do you know what imitation to use?

Here a little educated guesswork comes in. If it is early in the season, April and May, then unless you see an obvious hatch in progress, and the accompanying rise, expect the trout to be feeding from mid-water to the bottom. It is likely, because midge pupae and larvae

Top nymph-fisher Nigel Savage shows off a superbly conditioned rainbow trout from Rutland Water. This large, man-made reservoir grows-on some very big fish, both rainbow and brown trout, and many of them fall to well-presented nymphs. This was an early-season fish taken by light-line tactics in only a few feet of water. When hooked from the bank in such shallow water, rainbows of this class are capable of running out line well into the backing, and it is important that the reel you use has a free-running clutch. A reel which doesn't give line easily when a fish makes a surprise bolt courts disaster.

make up such a high proportion of a stillwater trout's diet, that these creatures will figure in the feeding pattern, even if the fish aren't taking them exclusively. So why not try a dark, weighted midge pupa and fish it deep? You may not be absolutely right, but the likelihood is that you will be close enough to catch a fish. A quick check with a marrowspoon will either confirm your suspicions or give a strong clue to a changed approach.

Stillwater trout feed heavily on both the larvae and pupae of the chironomid midge in the first couple of months of the season, often taking them just off the lake bottom. To fish midge pupae imitations at depths of up to 15ft, you need a specialized leader, though the rest of the tackle is standard. The rod should be 9½–10ft long and rated for an AFTM 6 or 7 line. This should be a floater, preferably with a weight-forward profile for distance casting; an important point if you are fishing from the bank, as you need the range to find the right depth.

The leader should be about 25ft long and made up of 5–6lb breaking-strain nylon. It should carry two droppers, spaced at 5ft and 10ft from the tip of the leader. With a weighted midge pupa on the point and two lighter versions to the droppers, an effective three-fly cast is created which will cover fish from the bottom to 10ft up in the water. Various patterns may be used for this point fly: the Deep Buzzer, Epoxy Buzzer, Wire Buzzer and Blakeston's Buzzer; indeed, any midge pupa imitation which is weighted to sink quickly.

The other two patterns should also be midge pupae imitations, but in different colours and much lighter. Using three weighted flies on a very long leader is asking for tangles. The intention is to use the heavily weighted point-fly to sink rapidly to the bottom, straightening the leader and allowing all three flies to fish at the correct depth, but you need the leader to land relatively straight in the first place.

This is not a technique for windy conditions, especially if you have little experience of casting with ultra-long leaders. Try to find a sheltered spot, preferably where you can cast into water 10–15ft deep. A headland or point is an ideal location, especially in a light breeze. Use an open loop in casting to get the flies out to the correct range. Long leaders don't take kindly to a tight, upright casting style so to keep tangles to a minimum, drop the rod slightly to the side on the back-cast, thereby opening up the loop. Then allow the back-cast to turn over fully before you make the forward cast; slowing your casting style a little will help.

On the final forward cast and shoot, as the line has almost fully turned over on to the water, tug it back slightly; this has the effect of turning over the long leader, preventing it falling back on itself. This is further helped by the weighted point-fly with its increased momentum. Once both line and flies have landed, and you are happy that the leader has not landed in a heap, make any necessary mend in the line to prevent it being dragged round in the breeze and then simply wait for the flies to sink.

ABOVE Nigel Savage shows the typical casting style needed with long leaders. Instead of using an upright rod position, and the tight loop it produces, the angler lays the rod more to the side during the back-cast, which opens up the loop of line and prevents the flies catching on the leader. It is a technique used by many stillwater anglers, as it allows them to cast long distances even with a team of three flies. On the forward cast the rod is brought into a more upright position before the final haul and shoot. Feathering the line, or even tugging it back slightly as it shoots out over the water, further assists the long leader to turn over correctly.

RIGHT A large reservoir rainbow bolts after picking up a small sub-surface nymph. Fish of this size and power test a light-line set-up to the limit.

This may take a minute, or more, even with little surface drag to move the line. If the breeze is sufficient to move the line, put an upwind mend in it as soon as a bow begins to form. This reduces the drag effect of the wind and prevents the flies from moving too fast and rising in the water. This is important, for fish mopping up chironomid pupae respond best to a fly fished as slowly as possible. Some may say 'static', but considering the motion caused by sub-surface currents, this is unlikely. The fact is that sub-surface water movement can impart life into an imitation, so it is a bonus in fooling the fish. What is not a bonus is too much surface drag. This speeds up the movement of the fly, even if you are retrieving very slowly, and diminishes the imitation's effectiveness.

Having located a concentration of feeding fish, you may have a take a cast, though even they may not always be easy to detect. Confident, sail-away takes do happen but often nothing more than a slow tightening is apparent, or even only a twitch of the line. These latter takes are often difficult to spot in broken water, but in calm conditions quite delicate line movements can be seen even at range. Don't mistake a small stab of the line-tip for a tentative pull, for you rarely feel a take when fishing in this manner. These fish are confidently mopping up any midge pupae they see, and that includes your fly. The gentle takes produced should be met by a solid lift of the rod.

In rough weather, all too often a problem in early-season fishing, a switch to a sinking line may be necessary. Many small invertebrates are disturbed when a good wave is pounding the shore, and as long as the water doesn't become too coloured, the trout move in

Bardon's Hare's Ear nymph is tied short to produce a small fly for selective feeders, while still using a hook large enough to cope with a powerful reservoir rainbow.

They don't come much better than this fin-perfect Farmoor rainbow. One fortunate aspect of nymph fishing is that it often tempts the better-quality fish, especially if those around you are fishing with lures. Grown-on fish are usually more wily than their recently stocked counterparts, and a small nymph fished in a natural manner often proves their undoing.

to feed on the rich pickings. Their feeding is not usually targeted toward a specific creature, but is more general. Here, more suggestive nymph patterns come into their own; large, buggy creations which sink quickly and imitate anything and nothing. A big weighted Hare's Ear Nymph, a large Pheasant Tail, a Glass Nymph or a Montana all work well as a point-fly. On waters with a good caddis-fly population, trout often pick up the large, cased larvae as they trundle along the bottom. The fact that the succulent body of the caddis larva is covered in an indigestible coating of sand or small stones doesn't seem to bother the fish, which scoop them up, cases an all. Suitable imitations such as the Cased Caddis, Van Klinken's Caddis or a Stick Fly are taken with equal enthusiasm provided they are fished slow and deep.

In rough, cold weather, when conditions preclude the use of a floating line, a sinking line such as an intermediate or a Wet Cel II is effective. In very windy conditions wave action drags a floating line around far too much, removing any possibility of a controlled retrieve. A sinking line cuts quickly through any surface drift, allowing the flies to be inched along the bottom.

Here a 9½ft rod rated for a 7 or 8 line is perfect. The line, matched to the rod, should be a weight-forward, its density depending on the depth of water to be fished. But err on the lighter side, as it helps maintain a slow retrieve rate without constantly catching the bottom. Leader length should be kept to a minimum. In a brisk blow, long leaders are out. Instead, keep to a manageable 12ft, cutting back if you experience too many tangles. In rough conditions, especially if the water is slightly coloured, a shorter leader is no disadvantage. A three-fly cast of 5–6lb breaking-strain nylon is about right, though it may be reduced to only two flies or even a single fly if conditions dictate.

Fly choice usually begins with a weighted point-fly, the two droppers being smaller and lighter, sizes 12 or 14 being ideal. Even if the fish are not taking the large point-fly, which is unusual, the two smaller nymphs, such as a small

Insect hatches become less prolific in the lowering temperatures of autumn, and the fish switch from regular surface-feeding to grubbing around on the bottom for creatures such as shrimps and hog-lice. Then a large weighted nymph can be worked slowly along the bottom on an intermediate sinking line or a floating line and a long leader. This is a deadly method at both ends of the season. The fly should be allowed to sink well before the retrieve of slow, short draws or a simple figure-of-eight is started. Spring and autumn trout are rarely willing to chase a quickly moved fly, and the slow, steady approach pays. Here Charles Jardine has hooked a good stillwater rainbow at range and has almost played it out.

Hare's Ear Nymph, a Pheasant Tail Nymph or a couple of spider patterns, give the fish alternatives. The point-fly is still useful in acting as an anchor, sinking the leader quickly and aiding presentation.

Nymphs usually need to be retrieved. Even when they are allowed to drift free, a slow figure-of-eight retrieve is needed to prevent the line becoming slack and to keep in touch with the flies. Other effective retrieves include a slow 6in draw, repeated, and a shorter, quicker twitch, which often induces a fish to take. Accelerating the rate of retrieve often tempts a following fish into grabbing hold. Just as often, though, the fly is picked up as it sinks back after a quick pull. Unfortunately, with no hard-and-fast rules, these various methods of retrieve rate need to be experimented

with on a day-to-day basis. However, a slow, steady retrieve is usually the most effective.

Presentation depth is crucial, and the closer to the surface the flies are fished, the more crucial it becomes. They must be where the trout are, which may be in the surface film, on the bottom, or somewhere in between. Exactly where is all part of the puzzle. Fortunately, clues are there. As the water warms, and the insect hatches become more regular, the trout feed closer to the surface. They don't always reveal their presence by rising, but insect hatches can indicate what the trout are doing a few feet down.

Given a hatch of olives, caddis or chironomids with few fish rising, the likelihood is that the trout are concentrating on the nymphs or pupae some distance

LEFT A warm summer's day and a gentle ripple; ideal conditions for nymph fishing on a reservoir. This is picturesque Eyebrook Reservoir on the Northamptonshire/Leicestershire border. The angler is left-handed, so a breeze blowing right to left is perfect for him. For right-handers a wind blowing in the opposite direction, on this day to be found on the far bank, is the best option. Casting at an angle of between 50 and 80 degrees across the wind allows a gentle curve to build in the line as it drifts downwind. So long as the drift is gentle, and doesn't move the line too fast, it brings the flies round in a steady arc. By casting 25yd or more and gradually working along the bank, the angler can cover a great deal of water and a lot of fish.

This superb reservoir rainbow fell to a size 16 Hare's Ear Nymph fished just beneath the surface. The fish had been feeding heavily on small chironomid pupae in clear, shallow water, making the sub-surface rise-form typical of a fish taking pupae and nymphs just before they emerge as winged adults. This necessitated the use of a light rod and leader. Fish feeding in this manner can be extremely selective when it come to pattern size. It is all too easy to use a larger fly than necessary; chironomid pupae are slim and delicate. If anything, err on the small side – it will be more productive. Also, ease into a take rather than simply striking. A full-blooded thump will only snap the leader or pull the small hook free.

below the surface. A relevant imitation or team can be set up and the water fished methodically until takes occur. Another ploy is to use more general nymph patterns in the hope of deceiving a fish. This fish can then be spooned and its feeding pattern determined. A small Pearl-ribbed Hare's Ear, Four Water Favourite or a Gold Bead Pheasant Tail are all excellent choices. A combination of patterns tied on size 10, 12 and 14

Nymph fishing can also be successfully employed from a drifting boat, particularly when the fish are feeding near the surface. The cast is made either straight down or slightly across the wind, fishing either blind or casting to rising fish working their way up the ripple. The tackle set-up of an AFTM or 7 rod and a floating line works just as well from the boat as it does from the bank, and with only water behind the angler, long leaders are much easier to cast. Here Nottingham angler Bob Carnill has tempted an Eyebrook rainbow into taking a Suspender Buzzer fished just in the surface. One word of warning: If you are using a long leader, make sure that the top dropper isn't tied so far away from the point-fly as to make netting a fish impossible!

hooks is a good starting point, remembering to use the largest fly in the team on the point. The tactic should be much the same floating line approach as for early-season nymph fishing, though as you won't be fishing so deep, you don't need as heavy a point-fly.

Given obvious surface activity, the assumption may be that a switch to dry fly is necessary. But take a long, hard look at the rise-form. Trout often target pupae and nymphs only an inch or so below the surface, but the resultant disturbance can look almost like a proper surface rise, with the trout's back and tail breaking surface. What isn't seen is the trout's nose: that remains beneath the surface where the food is.

If this type of rise is suspected, switch to a team of small, lightweight nymph patterns. Trout feeding in this manner are often difficult to tempt, so the key is to fish patterns which sit at the perfect level. Leadbetter's Suspender Buzzer, with its buoyant foam thorax, is ideal, as are the Mobile Buzzer and the Foam Shipman's. Again, try to find out the size and type of food being taken. Often

a size 14 is small enough, but if much smaller insects are being taken, then this must be reflected in pattern size.

In really calm conditions, especially when the water is clear, trout can become preoccupied with very small chironomids, insects best imitated on size 20 or 22 hooks. These fish were formerly considered uncatchable, but scaling-down hook-size and tackle makes them eminently catchable, though never easy. Using tiny midge pupae patterns, such as the Herl Buzzer, Hotpoint Buzzer or a small and versatile Hare's Ear Nymph dressed on a size 16 or 18 hook, can transform a frustrating day into a thrilling one. But tackle must be scaled down accordingly. An 8 ft AFTM 4 or 5 rod is in keeping with this style of fishing. Leader strength should be reduced to 3lb breaking-strain or less, and the tactic of degreasing the leader becomes imperative. Tackle such as this is capable of landing a big fish, and prevents the pull-outs and crack-offs which may be experienced with a heavier rod and a small hook and light leader.

A shallow flat, dropping away into deeper water, is a prime spot at which to find fish feeding on chironomid pupae. Rutland regular Chris McKechnie is using a team of small midge pupae to tempt rainbows cruising just below the surface. The water is calm, making a delicate presentation extremely important, and regular degreasing of the leader is necessary to help the lightly tied pupae cut quickly through the surface film. While very calm water can hamper presentation, the advantage is that takes are easy to spot. By crouching low, the angler can see the merest twitch on the leader as a fish picks up the fly. In shallow, weedy margins, Chris uses his landing-net as a line basket, preventing loose coils snagging drowned plant stems and helping the line to shoot easily.

FACTFILE

Standard tackle for stillwater nymph fishing includes a rod 9–10ft long rated for an AFTM 6–7 weight line. This line should be either a floater or of an intermediate density. By using a long leader of up to 20ft and varying the size and weight of the point fly being used, a nymph, or indeed a team of nymphs, may be fished from the lake bottom to the surface.

The retrieve rate should be generally slow from a series of short draws to a steady figure-of-eight, to almost static where the line simply drifts around with the breeze. However, if fish are merely nipping the fly, the addition of either a series of rapid twitches on the line or a single long strip can often induce a finicky fish into grabbing hold.

The size of nymph pattern to be used also varies considerably, depending on the prey species apparent at the time. This can mean using anything from a damselfly nymph at over an inch in length to a tiny midge pupa at almost ⅛in.

or by folding the sticky-backed type over the line. Because they are buoyant, they allow a fly or team to be suspended beneath and drifted on the breeze. Sight-bobs may be fixed to the leader at any point and, being buoyant, hold the fly at a specific level, preventing it sinking further. Once the angler has worked out the trout's feeding depth, an artificial can be worked continuously in the killing zone.

The use of a sight-bob is deadly when trout want a free-drifted pattern at a definite level. The fly comes to rest naturally at just the right depth at every cast. Takes, indicated by a movement of the bob, range from a dramatic sail-away to the merest twitch, even a slight slowing of the drift. In fact, any movement of line or bob not in keeping with the normal drift-rate should be reacted to as if it is a take.

A river ploy which is becoming increasingly popular on stillwaters is the use of sight-bobs. These are small, castable bite-indicators made from foam so that they float on the surface. They come in fluorescent colours which makes them highly visible, even at long range, and are fixed to the leader either with a small stopper

A foam sight-bob of the fold-over type. Though frowned upon by some, buoyant sight-bobs certainly make fishing a weighted nymph at a specific level much easier. For example, if you want your nymph to fish 3ft down, simply set the indicator at 3ft from the fly, cast and let the fly work by itself. What is more, a take gives a visible indication on the sight-bob, which is easy to see even from 25–30yd. By using a weighted fly, a stop-knot and a sight-bob which slides up the line, it is possible to fish a fly 20–30ft down, suspending it just off the bottom. It is considered so deadly a method that some waters have banned its use.

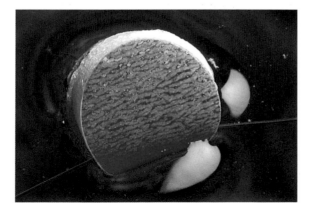

STILLWATER DRY-FLY FISHING

Dry-fly and emerger techniques have taken the still-water trout-fishing scene 'by the throat' in recent years. Where once the mere mention of having fished a dry fly on a reservoir or lake was enough to have you branded a crank, today the technique is probably the most effective catcher of trout.

What triggered this dramatic turn-around? Two things really: a better understanding of the food-forms of the stillwater trout, and how they are taken; and the realization by a number of skilled fly-fishers that trout would take a dry fly even when no obvious rise was taking place.

When anglers first turned to dry-fly fishing on still-waters they used river patterns, stiff-hackled dressings with upright wings which imitated the various species of ephemerid or olive found on running water. Flies such as these are intended to ride high on the surface to counteract the swamping effect of flowing water. But quite the opposite properties are needed in a stillwater dry fly. Stillwaters have relatively few ephemerid species, and where they do occur, their seasons are short, so it isn't surprising that standard dry-fly patterns work only at specific times of the year. What stillwaters do have, however, are chironomid midges in abundance.

The chironomid is part of a huge family of aquatic insects, all similar in form and habit, but varying in size and colour. These small, insignificant-looking insects form the cornerstone of stillwater dry-fly fishing; and it is their vast numbers which make them so important.

Apart from the chironomid, the lake olive, *Cloeon simile*, is another major trigger of a rise. On a warm summer's day, particularly in late morning, freshly hatched duns are often seen drifting along in the breeze, their upright wings making them look like small sail-boats. A dry olive often works well at such times, and a specific imitation such as Duck's Dun is tremendously effective. Because it sits low and has a natural 'footprint', the trout seem to like it almost as much as the real thing.

LEFT An autopsy reveals that this rainbow had been feeding on a mixture of chironomid pupae and coarse-fish fry. Curiously, trout feeding on small fry can be fooled by a well-presented dry fly, especially in shallow water. For this reason dry fly is a good technique for tempting trout which are feeding hard on needle-fry, a notoriously difficult preoccupation to beat.

Orange Adult Midge

Carrot Fly

CDC Emerger

Claret Bob's Bits

Amber Hopper

Blushing Midge

Two-tone Shipman's Buzzer

Foam Shipman's Buzzer

Hard-bodied Shuttlecock

This superb Chew Valley rainbow took an Orange Emerger. It had been feeding on emerging brown chironomid midge pupae around 5mm long. Trout taking midge pupae at this stage prove real 'suckers' for an orange-based fly.

Trout are catholic in their tastes and take whatever food is available in terms of numbers and ease of capture. Chironomids are only small, but the average stillwater contains literally millions upon millions of them. They are also exceedingly vulnerable, particularly when trapped on or in the surface film.

A typical chironomid hatch sees the pupae rising *en masse* to the surface and hanging there briefly before transposing into winged, sexually mature adults. The time varies, depending on conditions, from a few seconds to minutes. Calm weather causes the insects real problems, as the surface tension increases, due to the stillness and build-up of dust particles.

Degreasing the leader always pays in calm conditions, whether fishing from bank or boat. With little breeze to ruffle the water, the surface film builds up to such a degree that a nylon leader fails to sink unaided, making a disturbance pattern which puts the fish off. A compound such as Xink or Perma-sink applied regularly to the leader solves the problem and, in very calm conditions, it should be used after every two casts.

LEFT Not all lake olives are eaten by trout and birds. This one has fallen prey to a male common blue damselfly. Damsels provide a significant proportion of the trout's diet in summer. Usually it is the large nymphs which are taken, but at certain times the adults, flying low over the surface, or laying their eggs, fall prey in good numbers. An imitation of the bright blue male, tied with a detached deerhair body, is often effective at such times.

The prize. Careful presentation and the correct pattern can result in superb specimens such as this near 4lb rainbow. Fin-perfect trout such as this provide the cream of dry-fly sport on our lakes and reservoirs. That tail is put to good use when the fish is hooked, propelling it for as much as 50yd in a series of dazzling runs.

Then the pupae take a long time to break through and are trapped against a spongy wall, completely at the mercy of any cruising trout. Some pupae become exhausted by their efforts to break through and are soon mopped up as they hang twitching at the surface.

Observing the confident, sub-surface rise-forms trout make when feeding in this way, and when they are taking emerging and hatched adult chironomids, the first stillwater dry-fly fishers realized that what was needed was not a pattern which stood high and proud but one which sat low, right in the surface film, in the same way as the natural. And so, the stillwater dry fly was born: not a densely hackled, winged pattern, but a sparse, ragged fly that uses its body as much as its hackle to keep it afloat.

But pattern alone doesn't fully explain the success of stillwater dry-fly and emerger techniques. As in so many other fly-fishing disciplines, it is presentation that holds the key. With dry fly it is how leader and fly perform which is absolutely crucial, and on stillwaters success is achieved by means of two opposing properties. The fly must float, but its light or even non-existent hackle calls for an exceptional flotant. Gehrke's Gink, which comes in semi-liquid form, is perfect for the job.

Being viscous, it is easy to apply with the finger-tips, either to the whole fly or to only part of it. The latter point is important, as it allows an emerger pattern to hang in the surface film by the thorax, with the abdomen projecting beneath.

But while the fly must float, the leader must sink if it is not to create a tell-tale pattern in the surface which will cause a trout to shy away. This is especially important in calm, sunny conditions, and even in a good ripple, which does disguise surface disturbance somewhat, it is important repeatedly to degrease the leader to keep it sinking. This may be accomplished either with a proprietary degreaser such as Xink or Perma-sink, or by producing your own from a mixture of fuller's earth and washing-up liquid. Treatment with either helps the leader cut through the surface film, reducing its visibility dramatically.

Though the patterns used for dry-fly fishing on stillwaters vary considerably from those used on rivers, presentation and the elimination of drag are just as important on both. On rivers the problem is obvious. A fly is cast upstream and slightly across the flow and eventually it drags ineffectively across the surface as the current whips the line downstream. On stillwaters the problem is difficult to detect, but it can be just as disastrous.

Trout will often take a dry fly only when it is either static or allowed to drift freely downwind as if it were a natural insect. Casting directly into the wind does not bring a problem, as the fly comes back naturally on a slack line. However, a fly cast across the wind, either from bank or boat, fishes unnaturally as soon as surface drift draws the line tight. It may not drag perceptibly, but it does not drift correctly and this cuts the offer rate dramatically. This drag can be alleviated by using the river-fisher's technique of casting a snaky line, so that a few yards of natural drift occur before the curves are drawn out and the fly drags. This can be accomplished either by giving the rod-tip a wiggle just before the flies alight on the surface or by kicking the line back with the retrieving hand on the forward cast, causing the flies to jerk back a few feet and preventing the leader landing in a straight line, again with the same drag-free

ABOVE It's not only rainbows which fall victim to the dry fly. Large browns, such as this five-pounder, often find a well-presented dry fly to their liking. Late summer, when the weather is cooler, is a good time to find brown trout indulging in surface-feeding. Evening and early morning are also effective periods, when the light levels are low.

In calm, sunny conditions trout often keep their heads down during the heat of the day, but sunset, as the amount of light penetrating the water is reduced, is often the time for a spectacular rise. Evening is also the time for the caddis- or sedge-fly to hatch, and splashy, violent rises may indicate that the trout are taking emerging sedge pupae or freshly emerged adults. If adults are the prey, a dry fly such as the Elkhair Caddis or a small Muddler, skated over the surface, can produce spectacular action.

The angle of the light often causes problems in seeing takes at long range when glare makes surface visibility difficult. Polaroid spectacles reduce glare and are a definite advantage. They also help combat eye-strain. But sometimes even they are not enough, and here, top fly-fisherman Jeremy Herrmann is keeping low to take full advantage of the change in contrast on the horizon.

A trout's eye-view of an Orange Hare's-ear Emerger, with only the picked-out thorax caught in the surface film. The duller abdomen hangs below mimicking the midge's pupal shuck. This is achieved by applying flotant only on the thoracic region. The disturbance pattern formed by the leader on the surface can be eliminated by repeated degreasing of the nylon.

action. Advantages and disadvantages exist for both. Faster-action rods deliver line at a greater speed and pick up more quickly, allowing rising fish to be covered rapidly and accurately. The more decisive action also helps the line cut across the wind better, with less deviation. The softer-action rod may be slower, but is preferred by some as it is more forgiving on the light leaders often necessary for this style of fishing.

The configuration of the leader depends much on conditions and the number of flies being fished. With a standard team of three flies, 16ft of 5lb breaking-strain nylon is ideal. It is long enough to give good presentation, but not so long as to make accurate casting awkward. Droppers should be spaced at 5ft intervals back from the point-fly. This enables the line to be retrieved far enough to allow the fish to be brought to net without the top dropper catching in the tip ring.

Leader strength can be reduced to as little as 3lb breaking-strain in very calm conditions, and its length increased to more than 20ft. However, if the fish are

A warm summer's day, a nice wave and an ideal time to use dry fly. The angler on the bow has seen a fish rise and is covering it as it heads upwind. When a boat is drifting quite fast, the art is to judge how quickly the trout is moving in relation to the boat and to intercept it by casting a few feet upwind of its path. A slightly slack line helps, so that the fly remains static as the boat, and the line, drift on. Watch out for delicate takes. If you lose sight of your fly and a fish rises in the near vicinity, lift steadily. It may be your fly it has taken!

result. Suitable tackle for stillwater dry-fly and emerger fishing is 9½–10ft rod rated for an AFTM 6 or 7 line in conjunction with a matched weight-forward floating fly-line. A double-taper profile may be used, but the shooting properties of a weight-forward line are an advantage at long range.

The preferred rod-action is either a fast, progressive-action, of the American style, or a slightly softer middle proving difficult and taking only when a fly is placed right on the nose, then accuracy takes precedence. Now it is a good idea to change to a single fly, particularly if the still air makes casting a long leader troublesome.

Braided leaders, or those constructed from steeply tapered nylon, help the fly turn over correctly, the taper transferring the energy of the cast right through to the fly. And, because only one fly is being fished, the leader can be much shorter – 12ft is adequate – enabling fish to be picked off at up to 30yd.

The number of fly patterns used for this style of fishing is large and growing. Among the most effective are the Hopper, Bob's Bits, the Carrot Fly, the Raider, Shipman's Buzzer, the Shuttlecock, and the Cul-de-canard Emerger. A number, such as the Hopper, Raider and Shipman's Buzzer, are tied in a range of colours and sizes to suit conditions.

A variety of colours will work well throughout the normal season. Claret and black are both excellent during April and early May and then later on, when the predominant chironomid species are smaller and darker than during summer. Olive, cinnamon and natural hare's fur can be good mid-season alternatives, when similarly coloured naturals are on the wing. That said, red and orange are probably the two most deadly colours for dry-fly and emerger patterns. Few adult midges occur in either colour, but a phenomenon during the emergence of the adult chironomid may explain this apparent anomaly. At the very moment when an adult midge pulls free of its pupal shuck, it flushes

A fit summer rainbow provides spectacular action, especially when hooked on light tackle. In calm, clear water, scaling down to a leader of only 3lb breaking-strain can make the difference between success and failure, and a few heart-stopping moments will result as a fish thrashes at the surface. A light leader calls for a correspondingly lighter rod, perhaps as low as an AFTM 5 or even 4. Failing that, a rod with a softish, through action should be used. It may not be as quick and accurate as a stiffer rod, but it may save a frustrating crack-off.

The Raider is one of the new breed of stillwater dry flies. It is a sparse pattern intended to sit low in the surface imitating an emerging chironomid midge.

A healthy wind-lane caused by counter-rotating currents is a sight to gladden the heart of any stillwater fly-fisher. It concentrates insects and drowned terrestrials into a narrow area, a fact which the trout quickly recognize. Wind-lanes provide a focus for the angler and usually produce a few fish even on difficult days.

Cul-de-canard feather is the key to the Shuttlecock's effectiveness. While the oily feather holds in the surface film the fly's body and thorax hang seductively beneath.

Polypropylene is the winging material for the Polywinged Midge, an effective imitation of an adult or emerging midge.

orange-red as blood is pumped through its wings to expand them. This burst of colour is noticeable even from a few feet away, indicating to both trout and angler that the chironomid is at the point of emergence. This flash of colour seems to act as a trigger to the feeding

trout, and patterns which are either totally orange or red sometimes prove devastatingly effective.

RIGHT The object of the trout's desire. A chironomid midge at the point of emergence from its pupal shuck, with the flush of orange visible in the wings as blood is pumped around to expand them. This orange flush is a trigger for the trout, and probably the reason why dry midge patterns with a touch of orange are so deadly. In this half-in/half-out state, the midge is extremely vulnerable and trout autopsies often reveal fish to have been feeding almost exclusively on this stage.

FACTFILE

A standard tackle set up for stillwater dry-fly fishing would include a rod 9–9½ft in length rated for a floating AFTM 6–7 weight line, though for calm conditions a 5 weight gives additional delicacy. The line profile can be either double tapered or weight forward, the latter being better for long-range work.

Dry flies may be fished either singly or as part of a team. The single fly tactic is especially effective during very calm conditions or when extreme accuracy is the key. By using a tapered leader, either of braided nylon with a monofilament tip, or a steeply tapered, monofilament type, the power of

the cast is transferred right through to the fly. This helps it turn over properly allowing the angler to place a fly right in the path of a cruising trout.

Whatever set is used for stillwater dry fly the correct use of both floatants and sinkants is probably the most crucial. Because of the terrible disturbance pattern created by nylon floating on a calm surface it is important that it is treated with a sinkant such as Gehrke's Xink, or a simple mixture of washing-up liquid and Fuller's Earth. Sinking the leader reduces the disturbance pattern and produces a more natural presentation.

8 RESERVOIR BANK FISHING

Bank fishing is the first choice of local anglers on many big reservoirs throughout England and Wales. It has its attractions: you can wander at will and see more natural fly-life than at other waters and the stock fish soon toughen up and begin to feed naturally, giving a feeling of wild fishing which no small stillwater fishery can offer.

Reservoir bank fishing is the natural pursuit of the nymph-fisher, the man who loves to imitate the hatching insect. But although nymph fishing is the most popular method, at times during the season dry fly and lure fishing can be the best approaches. The prolific chironomid, the trout's most common food, begins to hatch in numbers from mid-April, and from now the reservoir will be on song for the rest of the season as various other insects come and go. The chironomid is usually about in one form or another throughout the year. At the end of May the lake olives appear, and the wind-blown hawthorn flies. Then, in late June, the sedges and damsels hatch, and, finally, autumn brings craneflies (daddies) and the coarse-fish fry.

Rutland bank-fishing regular Bob Garrett, from Leicester, loves his nymph fishing and catches a lot of good fish from the shallows at the top of the North Arm, which is where this came from.

Mid-summer, and among tell-tale signs on the bankside reeds that show that damsels are hatching in good numbers are the empty shucks from which the olive and metallic-blue flies have emerged.

A stocked rainbow that went in during April at 1lb can be pushing 3lb by autumn. Such fish are in perfect condition and are much prized by regulars, but fish up to 2lb will be the normal catch.

Choosing a spot to fish is a priority. Try to get away from popular and crowded areas. Most anglers fish at the accepted 25yd from each other, but an area which has occasional, well-spaced anglers is better.

A headland, such as the point of a bay, is worth looking for. It allows fan casting over a larger fishing area than is possible on a straight bank. Added to that, the continuation of the headland as a shallow ridge beneath the water is a definite holding area for trout, especially early in the season and during evening.

Shipman's Stickfly

Pitsford Olive

Tinhead Daddy

Distressed Damsel

Grousewing

Black Glass Buzzer

CDC Dun

Jack Frost

Hawthorn Fly

The problem with a regimented line of anglers is the inevitable noise and disturbance they cause. This pushes fish out further and further from the bank as time passes, with the result that you may be casting into fishless water after the first hour or so. It is worth recalling what Izaak Walton wrote more than 300 years ago: 'I must learn to be quiet'. This discipline is as important today as it was then, and it is easier to prac- tise on your own. Trout that have not been frightened are easier to catch.

In April, the giveaway sign that a good hatch of chi- ronomids (buzzers) is beginning is when martins start swooping across the water, picking off the hatching flies. Tackle up with a floating fly-line and set up a long, fine leader of one of the new low-diameter nylons. A breaking-strain of 5lb is sufficient for the main length of the leader, taking in two droppers, with 4lb for the tip.

An effective nymph set-up for this time of year is a leaded pattern on the point, with a Hare's Ear variant, size 12, with a short olive marabou tail a good choice.

Which fly? Brightly coloured lures are out when the hatch is on, but the upper leaf of the box has plenty of buzzers to choose from. An emerger fished in the film might be the one to try.

It's early May, and this fly-fisher is on Rutland's North Arm, during a prolific hatch of chironomids, with the swifts swooping to take their share. Trout, too, are feeding well on the ascending pupae. It's time for an Olive Glass Buzzer Nymph, or perhaps a black version of the same pattern.

On the two droppers, fishing up from the bottom, tie on an Olive Glass Buzzer Nymph and a Black Glass Nymph, both size 12. These are such realistic looking artificials that they will fool even the most educated resident trout.

Now the presentation must be right. At this time, trout take buzzers during the morning and up to late afternoon soon after they leave their larval cases and become free-swimming. The buzzers are then weak and making only half-hearted attempts to ascend to the surface, and they are easy pickings for the trout, but mostly deep down. Dick Shrive used to say: 'The evening rise begins at 10am'. He was right, with the chance of taking fish higher in the water increasing as the day progresses, especially if the wind drops off.

Imagine you are on that headland with a light wind blowing from left to right. Perfect! You follow a long cast by a lengthy pause to allow the nymphs to sink well down and a slight curve forms in your floating fly-line as you begin to retrieve. Now concentrate, watching for the fly-line to straighten and telegraph a take. This is one good reason for having a visible fly-line, but it doesn't need to be fluorescent.

Chironomids are present from now to the season's end in October, and from mid-June to September the emerging buzzer can be fished with great confidence. Well-proven patterns are the Shipman-style emergers, Bob's Bits and various kinds of Cul-de-canard (CDC) buzzers.

A land-borne fly which seems to have multiplied greatly in recent years is the hawthorn. This sizeable black, hairy-legged fly is best imitated on a size 12 hook. It appears on the reservoirs on windy days anytime after the first week in May according to weather conditions, and the trout become very keen on it. Have some good dry artificials at the ready, be observant, and when the time is right, fish a simple, single dry hawthorn pattern.

From mid-May until the first week in June many reservoirs have prolific hatches of pond and lake

Wading far out early in the season is unnecessary. All it does is push the trout out further. Being a good long-caster makes up for not wading. Wear only your 'wellies' and you can't wade far and are more mobile for walking. Here the landing-net is handy and is substituting as a line-tray.

Orange is a superb colour, especially during mid- to late summer. Add the sparkle of a silver bead and you have the Orange Silverhead.

olives. These delicate upwinged flies are well imitated with a single Cul-de-canard Olive dry fly, and a tiny nymph imitation also catches well. The artificial should be tied sparsely on a size 14 hook. A nymph we created with dyed olive hare's ear especially for Pitsford reservoir seems to work everywhere. Known as the Pitsford Olive, its dressing is simple.

Hook: Sizes 14–16.
Tying silk: Olive.

LEFT Nymph-caught fish in May are beginning to come into good condition.

BELOW This golden-bellied trout shows that browns, too, are now worth catching.

A landing-net can efficiently gather a floating line ready for an easy, non-tangle cast. A net with a spike at the end of the handle is perfect for this purpose.

Tail: A few strands of olive hen hackle-fibres.
Body: Dyed olive hare's ear fibres dubbed on to a fine copper wire.
Thorax: Olive Antron; shellback, buff-coloured feather-fibre.
Head: Clear varnish.

A few reservoirs, such as Ladybower and Tittesworth in the southern Pennines, do have a mayfly hatch, but most do not. But what does happen in June each year is every bit as exciting as a mayfly hatch. Then clouds of blue and olive damselflies hatch in the bankside weed-beds.

Because the damsel nymph is large and a strong swimmer with a wiggle-tail action, it is the fly-tyer's dream, enabling him to create an artificial on hooks as large as size 10 or 8 longshank. Both leaded and unleaded patterns are 'musts' for different tactical approaches.

If no damsels are hatching, a leaded pattern can still be fished with confidence, provided the natural has been about for a week or so. Fish it on a floating line and long leader so that it can be brought along the bottom. Twitch-twitch retrieves are good, inducing takes when long pulls fail.

But the most exciting of all is to see the damsels mating, with the metallic blue male and drab-olive female joined together and repeatedly dropping on to the water and taking flight again. Many don't make it as the trout respond, feeding confidently with great splashing rises. A slowly retrieved artificial blue adult damsel which floats is proving a new killing method.

A normal damsel hatch may take place on the hottest of days, and even in the middle of the day, and some trout are always interested in feeding on them. The nymphs swim across the surface to the bank or nearest reed-stem, crawl out and hatch in a few seconds. Don't be put off by the bright conditions and hot sun, but strip an olive damsel nymph quite fast just sub-surface. Jeanette Taylor's famous Olive Tinhead is deadly at this time.

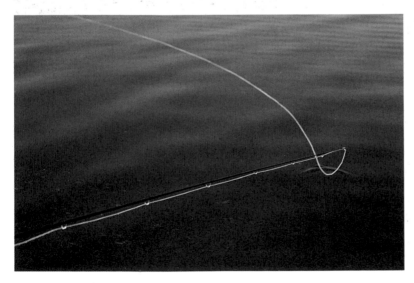

With a side-wind to drift a floating line and nymphs in an arc, all you need do is take up the excess slack with figure-of-eight retrieve.

ABOVE An alternative retrieve is a series of slow twitches, making the nymph dart 6in or so and then stop. On the pause grip the line with your index finger so as not to miss striking a take.

ABOVE Trout eat almost as many adult damsels as nymphs, so watch for this handsome creature being blown on to the water, especially when mating.

LEFT This rainbow trout of only 1½lb fell to an Olive Damsel Nymph. Spooning its stomach contents showed it had eaten more than 100 naturals.

It is mid-July before the best of the sedge fishing comes into its own. A hatch of sedge may begin at almost every reservoir in Britain as the wind dies to a light ripple during early evening and continues until about 10.30pm, when all goes quiet once more. Fish with one, two or three flies – that and what approach you use is up to you.

Find a well-sheltered area where a light ripple begins about 20yd out and the water is 6–12ft deep with weed-beds around. As the hatch of common silverhorn and grousewing sedges begins, you may see what seem to be a lot of trout rising for the adults. A closer look will reveal that the trout are few but rising continuously to take pupae from the surface film as they are about to hatch. If your casting doesn't disturb the fish, you may catch half-a-dozen in no time at all.

A good technique is to cast a single well-'Ginked' dry sedge, size 12, with a degreased sunk leader into the vicinity of the rises, usually on the edge of the ripple. Be patient and leave it there, and soon one of those feeding trout will find it and sip it off the top. This is a much better tactic than forever casting at rises and pulling back, causing a wake and scaring the trout.

Sub-surface nymph fishing, imitating that glutinous blob of tangled legs, wings and antennae which is the sedge pupa, can be practised successfully even when no rise is on, around 6p.m. for instance. Use a floating fly-line outfit as usual, with the same long leader, but this time put a size 10 lightly weighted Stick Fly on the point to imitate the bottom-crawling cased caddis grub or the sedge larva.

For the pupa patterns any combination of colours such as cream, yellow, pale green and brown have to be blended. The pupae on which the fish are feeding may be any colour, so check the stomach contents of the first fish caught. We used some new patterns with

RIGHT Newly hatched coarse fish pin-fry appear in their billions in late July/early August. Watch for trout attacking these shoals and use a size 12 Pearl or Silver Invicta dressed sparse.

BELOW In July, especially in the last two weeks, always stay on until dusk. It is then that a sedge rise is almost guaranteed in conditions such as these.

100

success on the Midlands reservoirs in 1994, such as Kevin Garne's Emerging Midge.

July is also the month when newly hatched coarse-fish fry, roach and perch appear in their millions in shallows and weed-beds along the banks. The trout's food chain is now at its peak, but they may still become pre-occupied from time to time with a specific food-form.

You may sometimes peer into the water to see what you thought was a shadow or weed-bed begin to move, and you realize that it is a shoal of pin-fry roach containing several millions of the little fish. If you stay quiet and keep watching, you may see a larger-than-average trout attack and temporarily scatter the shoal in no more than 2ft of water. Your pulse will race as you try and work out what tactic to use – but be warned, trout feeding like this are among the most difficult to tempt.

At least at this time of year the banks are rarely crowded and you have scope to stalk feeding fish instead of staying in one place. Several fry imitations are worth a try, and a size 12 hook is best. The Appetiser, Jack Frost and Sinfoid's Fry are worth a try, but a pure White and Silver Muddler is better, and a Silver or Pearl Invicta we found best of all in 1994. Again, you need only a floating line outfit.

The White and Silver Muddler is a superb pattern when trout are fry feeding. The head of spun white deerhair gives the fly a nice 'fishy' profile.

Autumn sees the larger coarse-fish fry about, and this is the time to try floating-fry patterns and larger lures. But what we all look forward to in early September are the first signs of the cranefly, or daddy-long-legs. If any one fly is guaranteed to bring large trout to take off the top, it is the daddy.

The crane fly, or daddy-long-legs, increases in numbers towards the end of August. These are the real thing and a matching artificial.

102

David Barker uses a line-tray home-made from a blown-up cycle inner tube. He likes to use floating-fry patterns in autumn.

This fine Chew brown was feeding on 2in-long roach fry.

Fish a simple Daddy artificial with the wind blowing from behind you, where, with luck, lots of naturals are hatching and being blown on to the reservoir. After a warm rain is best.

The sinking Daddy has become popular, but if ever a fly has been kept a close secret, it is the Daddy dressed on a size 10 tinhead hook. We are used to seeing and fishing Daddy imitations on the surface but trout still take them when they are well sunk.

Though originally designed as an imitation of a large, dark stonefly nymph, the Montana has been adopted as a general stillwater pattern. The fluorescent green-and-black coloration is deadly throughout the season.

F ACTFILE

For bank fishing you need a 7 or 8 floating line fished on a 9½–10ft fast-action fly-rod. Have faith in low-diameter nylons and polymers and carefully practise tying knots which are moistened with the lips before being pulled tight. The lighter you fish, the more takes you can expect.

Reservoir bank-fishing is a great challenge and has much to offer. It particularly suits season-ticket holders who fish short two- or three-hour sessions.

A few reservoirs don't have natural banks. These are known as concrete bowls, but they, too, are worth a try even if the water is deeper and perhaps needs a sinking fly-line.

RESERVOIR BOAT FISHING

Specimen wild brown and rainbow trout are always worthy fish to catch from a large reservoir. We refer to them as wild because they may have been stocked at no more than 1lb and may be well into double figures when caught. Occasionally one of these huge fish is hooked by a nymph-fisher, but form indicates that a large fish-imitating lure is the best artificial to offer. Grown-on fish are usually considered to be trout of 3lb upwards.

We chose two big reservoirs, Rutland Water (3,300 acres) and Grafham Water (1,500 acres), to try for these big fish. Each water has given marvellous sport over the years and doubtless will continue to do so.

Bank fishing for these big fish can be good at certain times, usually late on in the season, from the end of August until October. For season-through fishing it is better to fish from a boat, which gives more scope on these vast waters.

Specialized big trout hunting demands a few extra gadgets if you are to have complete control of your boat. First, to drift-fish effectively with a fast-sinking fly-line and a fish-imitating lure, it is necessary to have the boat drifting bow-first downwind. This can best be accomplished by putting a drogue out from the central stern position, but it is better to use a portable drift-control rudder. This is attached to the stern with a G-clamp and

Bank fishing is well worth a try for big trout, especially at the back end of the season. This fly-fisher's powerful outfit punches line into the wind, and he is using a line-tray in which to retrieve his line.

Bob Church checks his rudder before going out on Pitsford. The G-clamp is used to attach the rudder to the transom.

Black and Green Pretty

White Pretty

White Goldhead

Tandem Goldie

Sparkler Tube

Missionary

Ethafoam Fry

Datchet Rassler

Cat's Whisker

Light Bulb

An extension-dressed Appetiser, the perfect lure for fry-feeders, with (below) the longer dressing when dry. In the centre is the roach to be imitated. At the top of the hand is the same Appetiser lure when wet, which is how a marauding trout sees it. Imagine how it pulsates when cleverly retrieved!

operated by the angler who is sitting at that end of the boat. The boat drifts along sedately with the breeze and he tries to keep about 100yd from the shoreline over water 15–20ft deep.

A similar result can be achieved with the help of two 1m lengths of strong cord. The cord is used to tie each oar securely into the rowlocks, with the blades vertical. At the top of the drift the boat is turned to point the bow downwind and then the motor is cut. The boat continues to drift like this, allowing successful side-casting by both fishers. The tied-on oars stop the boat reverting to its natural broadside drift.

This bow-first drift technique was introduced by Dick Shrive and Bob Church and friends in the early days at Grafham, and it became known as the Northampton Style. It enables both fishermen to cast a sinking line from either side of the boat. The faster the line sinks, the deeper it fishes, and extra depth can be gained by feeding out slack line after a long cast.

Find the depth at which the trout are feeding, usually on or close to the bottom, and then retrieve by skimming the lures through at that level. The line is pulled round in an enticing, sweeping arc.

If the boat is drifting quickly in a strong wind, a slow retrieve does the trick, but if the progress is slow in a light wind, the retrieve may be speeded up. Takes are usually positive, but sometimes a big trout follows a lure and taps it several times, presumably with its head, before taking.

Anyone intending to search seriously for big reservoir trout does well to have a reliable anchor. Both Rutland and Grafham boats have good kedge anchors, but the length of the rope is nowhere near long enough for deep-water anchoring. We use 90ft of rope and 10ft of chain clipped to the anchor.

Why should we wish to anchor in deep water? Well, at Rutland during mid-summer, fry-feeding often takes place over depths of 40ft, with large trout chasing 6in fry up from the depths and making them leap in terror at the surface. It is then a question of who gets the meal first, the trout or the sea-gulls

Blakeman's White is part of a series developed by Tony Blakeman. It is tied with a heavily weighted under-body and a tiered, marabou wing. This configuration makes it a great pattern for fishing 'on-the-drop'.

A good, heavy anchor attached to 10m of chain and 30yd of rope. A winding board prevents the rope forever tangling.

Graham Pearson, from Leicester, prepares for a day on the rudder at Rutland Water, with his box of 6in-long fish-imitating lures to hand.

BELOW Graham uses his knee to keep the boat on its bow-first drift downwind. This is a well-known big-fish drift from the tower in the North Arm straight down the centre, where bottom features include a raised pipe.

which hover above the water in readiness. It is always worth anchoring at a spot where sea-gulls are working and diving on to the surface.

A big landing-net is vital for bringing a specimen trout safely on board. No other option is available unless you are fishing catch-and-release. Even then a quick weighing and photograph may be wanted.

A boat should be anchored from the bows in a big wind. It rides easily in this position and doesn't ship water. A long rope is needed to make a good anchor

Dead or dying roach fry up to 5–6in long on the surface have usually been chased by attacking trout. It's time to anchor-up and fish with a fish-imitating lure.

BELOW A large landing-net should always be at the ready. Here a big brown drops in nicely.

hold, and this imparts a lot of swing to the boat. Once you are used to this movement, it can be used to advantage to cover new water.

A stern anchor causes less swinging in lighter winds, and the boat remains almost stationary. This is important when an exact hotspot, such as an aerator tower or other submerged feature, has been identified.

The size of fish caught by this technique can be very rewarding, and these days we tend to keep the rainbows and return the browns, a trend which is slowly but surely catching on with most regular reservoir fishers.

LEFT Bob Wallinger, the Draycote Reservoir lure-fishing specialist, has taken some fine catches there from an anchored boat. Here he chooses a big Sparkler lure.

BELOW The reward for fishless hours: a fine Rutland brownie of 7lb 3oz.

LEFT Norman Bithell caught this 16lb grown-on rainbow from Hanningfield Reservoir, Essex. He was fishing from an anchored boat close to the rearing cages.

BELOW The Concrete Bowl gets its name from the fact that it works well on large, concrete-rimmed reservoirs. It has a mobile, marabou tail and may be fished from either boat or bank.

Bob boats a big Draycote rainbow to a Silver Sparkler lure.

Gold-coloured lures work particularly well with brown trout, a fact first recorded by Bob Church and Peter Gathercole in the early days at Rutland, when the Goldie Tandem lure was developed.

BELOW This time an Appetiser did the trick. It is seen with fry spooned from the rainbow's stomach.

FACTFILE

Tackle for fishing in this way is a powerful 10ft carbon rod, a Lineshooter wide-drum reel, and 100yd of 30lb flat, black pre-stretched nylon backing. The fly-line for fishing at great depth is improvized from 10yd of lead-core trolling line, the kind that comes in 100yd spools and has a colour-change every 10yd. We also use heads made from size 11 Hi-speed Hi-D lines and the Deepwater Express very fast-sink lines. Leader material is 4–5yd of 8lb nylon.

With a large landing-net and a choice of good lures, some sport is virtually assured. Proven size 6 or 8 tandem lures which have caught many big fish, including some in double figures, include the Appetiser, Goldie and White Muddler. Lightweight 4–6in tube-flies made from pearl Mylar bodies and with Crystal or Flashabou wings are also successful.

Single longshank hook lures should not be ignored, with the choice the same as for tandem patterns. Add a selection of long marabou-tailed Leadheads with painted eyes. Some are termed Tinheads (a fixed soldered head); others have weighted chain-bead eyes. Cat's Whisker, Light Bulb and White Pretty Dog (this last pattern varies in colour) are all good.

10 IRISH LOUGH FISHING

Fly-fishing for wild brown trout on the big Irish loughs is both tough and uncompromising, yet visitors are drawn annually from all over Europe. We have spent a lot of time in Ireland and have fished most of the major waters. But it is the four western loughs of Conn, Carra, Mask and Corrib which have cast their spell on us.

At more than 3,000 acres, Lough Carra is the smallest of the four loughs and roughly the same size as England's biggest reservoir, Rutland Water. It is a unique, shallow lough with a pure white bottom of calcified limestone. Fish to around 3¼lb are plentiful and can be taken on wet or dry flies. With fewer rocks showing, Carra is less dangerous than the other waters, allowing

long drifts over the middle. A 'secret' inner lake is hidden by 200m of thick reeds, but it can be reached and is very productive

Linked to Carra by the Keele River is Lough Mask. At 21,000 acres, it is both large and dangerous. It is also the most difficult to master, but it has given us our moments of glory and we always return. We now know the lough well enough to take a boat out on our own, but we still prefer to use an experienced gillie. For a start it's safer, because he knows the positions of submerged and dangerous rocks at various water heights. He also holds the boat perfectly on a drift with the use only of the pegged, back oar, keeping it over the best

Jeremy Herrmann (right) talks tactics with a visitor who had just finished a successful morning's fishing on Lough Carra. The white, calcified bottom to this lake is so rich that it resembles a coral sea. No wonder the trout grow big!

Adult Damselfly

Dabbler

Wet Mayfly

Murrough

Cock Robin

Goat's Toe

Detached Daddy

Golden Olive Bumble

Green Peter

fishing shallows for as long as possible. And an Irish gillie is always excellent company, with a fund of Irish tales to relieve the slack periods and to entertain during the traditional midday break on one of the islands while the Kelly's Kettle, or even one of the original Volcanoes, bubbles on the fire.

Lough Corrib is the giant of Ireland's western stillwaters and, at more than 40,000 acres, is massive. It has 365 islands, one for every day of the year, and is joined to Mask by subterranean streams which reappear at the little town of Cong on upper Lough Corrib, which means that salmon which enter the system at Galway cannot get through. Corrib has the earliest big chironomid hatch of any major water we know. The Irish call it the duckfly, and it starts in late March.

The weather begins to close in on Lough Mask, with a strong westerly threatening straight off the Atlantic. Dave Allen fishes on, waiting for a trout to lunge at his Bob fly.

BELOW It's early spring and the west of Ireland's Lough Corrib awakens. The first fly-fishers venture out at the end of March.

113

114

LEFT The fly that hatches so prolifically on Corrib early in the season is the black chironomid, known to the Irish as the duckfly.

BELOW The Ascending Midge Pupa was originally designed by Peter to imitate midge pupa on reservoirs and small lakes. However, in calm conditions at duckfly time, it is a deadly pattern on Irish loughs such as Corrib.

BELOW A cool spring breeze makes Bob Church wear a sheepskin waistcoat as he brings a fine wild Corrib brown to the gillie's waiting net.

ABOVE Lough Conn from Pontoon Bridge Hotel, with a boat working the shoreline.

RIGHT A good fish to artificial mayfly on Lough Conn.

Unconnected to these three loughs, but not far away is 14,000-acre Lough Conn, lying in the shadow of Mount Nephin. This 12-mile long lake has good boat stations at each end, at Crossmolina and Pontoon Bridge, where gillies can also be hired. Conn produces big fish quite regularly, and a few years ago we had a good catch which included a brace of 4lb and 3½lb.

Ballinrobe is a good centre from which to fish Carra or Mask, a friendly little town with plenty of guesthouses. We always stay with gillie Robbie O'Grady and his wife, Nan. For Corrib, Oughterard is a good centre.

Conn is perhaps best fished from Pontoon Bridge Hotel, with its boat moorings only yards away.

Corrib is without doubt the best choice for early-season fishing. We had a lovely catch during the last week of March, with the fish taken almost exclusively

LEFT A fine brace of wild browns from Lough Conn.

BELOW Salmon sometimes take a fly off the top on Lough Conn. Paul Harris looks decidedly happy.

on imitations of the large and abundant black chironomid. Various emergers on size 12 hooks worked well in a light breeze, but a Black and Silver Spider, also size 12, was deadly as the wind increased.

Black and Silver Spider. This simple pattern works well in a hatch of black midge, such as those found at duckfly time on the great Irish loughs.

All four waters have massive mayfly hatches in May, and although they are at their best for only one or two weeks, both Mask and Conn continue to have reasonable hatches through to August. In fact it was on August 6 on Conn a few years ago that we experienced one of the best mayfly hatches we have ever seen. It brought a combined catch of 22 brown trout, nearly all returned.

The lake olive is another species which begins to hatch on these waters in May. It is a lovely delicate

ABOVE With chironomids hatching in plenty and the wave a mere ripple, it pays to try a small black nymph rather than a big bushy wet fly.

RIGHT The proof: this Corrib brown trout had fed exclusively on duckfly pupae.

BELOW Come May, and the delicate, upwinged olives hatch and drift like miniature sailing-boats. The trout soon rise to them, and the swifts, swallows and martins share in the feast and confirm to the fly-fisher the extent of the hatch.

upwinged fly. But be warned, the trout on all these loughs sometimes becomes preoccupied in their feeding!

As summer progresses, so the big sedges appear, causing quite a disturbance as they skitter along the water surface. Known locally as murroughs, they are imitated on size 10 or 8 longshank hooks, some with a claret body tied in, others grey, brown or black. The olive version is the famous Green Peter. These flies are usually fished on the point or top dropper.

Towards autumn the cranefly or daddy-long-legs hatches bring the big fish up to feed. Mask boatman Jimmy Murphy was out with an English fly-fisher who landed a 13½lb brown on a daddy-long-legs. A year later he returned to fish again with Jimmy, but before they set out he told Jimmy he had brought an old friend

The Sooty Olive is an imitation of the lake olive, *Cloeon simile*, tied in the traditional Irish wet-fly style with a wing of bronze mallard.

LEFT It's traditional to go ashore on one of Corrib's 365 islands for a midday brew-up. The water comes straight from the lough.

to meet him. He opened the boot of his car and presented Jimmy with the same trout expensively set up in a case. It is in Jimmy's house to this day for all to see.

Many locals revert to a style of fishing known as dapping at both mayfly and daddy-long-legs time, using the natural insects. A long telescopic rod of around 15ft is used with a short length of blow-line (6ft is ideal) which at one end is tied to the reel line, which should be about 10lb breaking-strain nylon, and at the other to the leader, which should be about 6ft of 6lb nylon. A fine-wire size 10 hook completes the set-up.

Collecting the live insects is not difficult. A clear plastic container with breather holes is needed, and enough insects can be gathered from outbuildings, especially the daddies. Mayflies can be found

118

A Yellow Mayfly artificial did the trick even though the hatching natural is more olive than yellow.

Jimmy Murphy, a fine Lough Mask boatman, keeps his boat in Cushlough Bay. It was just out of the bay that his English guest caught this 13lb 8oz trout. He had it set up and presented it to Jimmy on his next visit.

120

resting in trees and bushes, but grasshoppers, if you can find them, are the best bait of all.

A good stiff breeze is needed for efficient dapping, usually considered a drifting-boat method. Lift the rod, pay out line until it is running out horizontally in the breeze, and then lower the rod so that the insect alights on the water before lifting the rod and repeating the process. The bait insect bobs along the waves and the trout virtually hook themselves, with no need for the angler to strike quickly. It is a deadly method in Ireland's loughs.

With its extensive shallows, Carra has big damselfly hatches, and it was here that we first saw how trout sometimes feed frantically on the adult blue damsels as they are blown off the reed-beds or as they are mating. The Goat's Toe artificial with its blue peacock breast-feather hackle brought us a good catch. The trouts' stomachs were full of blue adult damsels.

Each August Bank Holiday at Ballinrobe the World Wet Fly Championships see close on 600 fly-fishers competing in a five-day competition on Lough Mask. We have fished this event on many occasions and one year Bob missed first place overall by only a couple of ounces. It is a challenging competition, and the atmosphere is terrific.

If you go to fish Conn in early May, go out from the Pontoon Bridge end and go down a channel into adjoining little Lough Cullin. It is here in the shallow water that the first mayfly hatch, and the trout are fine 1½-pounders.

Bob Church boated this superb 3lb 4oz Lough Carra brown on an artificial daddy-long-legs.

Always have the gillie work the boat through the shallow, rocky areas of the lough. They are always good for a fish or two.

FACTFILE

The west of Ireland loughs have something special when it comes to untouched beauty. They are 'difficult' at times, but they are among the loveliest places you will ever fish.

The fishing is all by boat, preferably with a gillie of experience on the particular lough. A rod of at least 10½ft is needed, with an 11-footer even better. It should carry a size 6 or 7 floating line. Imitative patterns of the natural insects are by far the best to use – an approach much different from that needed for aggressive rainbows. The fishing is for really wild browns only, fish that have hatched naturally in the feeder streams. They are cautious, but most satisfying to catch.

Both Corrib and Mask produce wild browns into double figures each year to fly-fishers. They also produce many more to trollers using spoon baits.

SMALL FISHERIES

11

The last 20 years have seen the creation of many small trout fisheries of 1–50 acres all over Britain. They are stocked with good-sized rainbow trout of 1½lb upwards and most have a few double-figure fish which ensure plenty of interest among the regular rods. The chance of catching a specimen trout, wild or stocked, has a special appeal, and like them or frown on them, small-water trout fisheries are here to stay, playing a major part in our sport.

Although many anglers are motivated to try to catch a large trout from a small fishery, they do find some obstacles, chief of which on some fisheries is that the water is not clear enough to allow a sight of the fish and to allow it to be stalked. Only gravel-pits and the chalk-based waters of the south and Cotswolds have water clear enough to enable a big fish to be selected as a quarry and then carefully stalked. But spotting the fish in the first place is still an art. A pair of good quality polarized sunglasses is essential, and preferably an eyeshade hat as well.

Once the knack of spotting fish other than stock trout is acquired, you are halfway to catching that specimen of 10lb or more. Alan Pearson used to be a successful catcher of big rainbows on the small

This fly-fisher is well equipped for stalking trout. He can wander freely with his landing-net attached to his shoulder, and a large-brimmed hat and polarized glasses help him spot the fish. His rod is at the ready, armed with a single leaded nymph.

Nymph Glass Damsel

Bottom Scratcher

Green Beast

Spent Mayfly

Orange Cat's Whisker

Hi-spot lead nymph

Olive Tinhead

Viva Tinhead

LEFT Bob Church takes advantage of bankside cover to conceal himself from a cruising trout, and his leaded nymph 'plops' into the water.

ABOVE The fish is on, and Bob moves into a clear area to play and land the trout. But he still crouches low so as not to panic the fish.

BELOW It was a good fish, a brown of 5lb 2oz, typical of the trout Dever Springs produces in summer.

Hampshire fisheries, and he admitted he was helped by having remarkable fish-spotting vision. He earned the tag of 'X-Ray Eyes'! But this is the technique.

Walk slowly round the lake, concentrating your vision on the bottom. Watch for white, chalky, weed-free areas, because it is when they move over these that the trout can be seen best.

Once one of the bigger fish has been spotted, you then have to tempt it to take your fly (nymph). For this a reasonable selection of weighted nymphs and Tin-head-style Tadpoles is a must. A trout may be seen swimming past no more than a few inches off the bottom in 5–6ft of gin-clear water, and a non-weighted fly would never sink fast enough to intercept the fish. It would be long gone before such a fly could ever reach the correct depth.

The simple trick is to cast your weighted nymph carefully and well ahead of the trout's cruising course. This gives it time to sink deep down as the fish approaches. Then it's a matter of twitching the nymph and beginning a slow retrieve. You may see the take quite clearly as the trout opens its mouth, revealing a

Some fly-fishers use 'sit-and-wait' tactics at small fisheries, but they are not so effective as stalking.

flash of white jaw, and this enables you to make a perfectly timed strike and the fight begins.

If fish keep following your nymph and then shying away, then obviously they are suspicious of it. Change the colour, and perhaps the size, and try again. Allowing the nymph to rest on the bottom and moving it only when a fish appears is also a tactic which works well.

Another reason for refusal could be that you are fishing with too heavy a nylon leader. Try going lighter or using one of the low-diameter nylons. Always use a leader as light as you dare. That said, don't be silly and go too light and so risk being constantly broken.

Trout have a plentiful choice of food on which to gorge in summer, but when we spent a July day at Dever Springs in Hampshire with the top lady International fly-fisher, Jeanette Taylor, it was the damselfly which was most active. The damsel hatches in multitudes on hot sunny days, so keep a good supply of artificials in your fly-box and watch for the opportunity to use them.

The Orange Lead Bug is a small heavily weighted pattern designed for casting to trout which are being stalked. Its high visibility is attractive to trout and an advantage to the angler.

Varying the retrieve can make the difference between success and failure, and it should be done to suit the fish's mood on the day. Many anglers use a figure-of-eight retrieve, but short, fast twitches can be good, and late in the day stripping the fly in may make an extra-wary fish take.

Jeanette decided to fish at long range as algae clumps bubbled up to float on the surface close to where she was casting. Keeping to her favourite pattern, one which she invented, a size 10 Olive Tinhead Nymph which imitates a damsel nymph, she felt the better fish had moved out as it was nearly midday and a lot of lines had been cast. She was fishing blind, but her woman's intuition was working spot on, and she soon struck into what was to prove the heaviest rainbow of the day, a fine 12½-pounder.

A few good brown trout were showing every so often, though the rainbows were much more prolific. It was a case of stalking in the real

RIGHT Here comes a cruiser, this time a decent-sized rainbow.

BELOW Jeanette covers it with an Olive Tinhead, and a few minutes later a 12lb 8oz rainbow is hers.

sense, watching and waiting patiently before casting, but before long I had a fine brace on the bank for a collective weight of more than 10lb. My successful pattern was a Hare's Ear Nymph variant with a black marabou tail, and, yes, it was well weighted.

Dever can produce really good sport to dry-fly. Earlier in the season, in late May, a best-ever brace for Bob

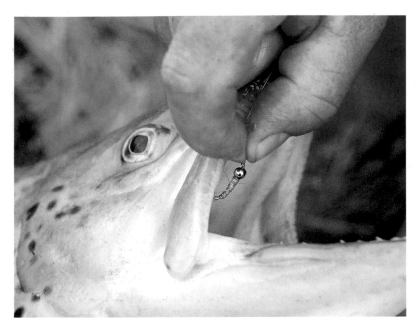

A specimen brown trout has a very large mouth. A size 10 Silver Head Nymph appears tiny in comparison.

BELOW Peter Cockwill is a small-fishery specialist, using the stalking technique and picking out a big fish every time.

during mayfly time was a fish of 16lb 1oz to mayfly nymph in the morning and then a fine fish of 12lb 9oz to a dry mayfly after tea, a memorable catch. The only other surface fly which brings fish up with any confidence is the daddy-long-legs during autumn.

Peter had been busy with his camera during our day with Jeanette, but at last he could no longer resist trying for one of the now shy rainbows moving in and out of a shallow corner of Dever's smallest lake. It was a good fish, but not a big double, but Peter couldn't tempt it. Then we saw why. It had a big nymph stuck to its bottom jaw, left after someone had been broken earlier in the day. No wonder it refused to take!

Mayfly nymphs are to be found on many of the smaller trout fisheries. The Nymphglass Mayfly nymph uses a layer of transparent Nymphglass to give added translucency.

Jeanette Taylor with a rainbow of 7lb and Bob Church with one of 11lb 8oz. The summer fish at this type of fishery are of good quality and ideal for the smoker.

ABOVE A fine small-fishery rainbow in the net. Few small fisheries allow catch-and-release as the fish fight almost to the death and many would die if returned.

RIGHT Peter Gathercole with his heaviest-ever brown trout at 11lb. It came from prolific Dever Springs in Hampshire.

FACTFILE

To fish for big trout in small waters, use a rod of 9–10ft with a floating line of sizes 6 to 8. A sink-tip or intermediate line can be useful, or even a medium sinker early in the season. The key factors are always the ability to spot fish, the use of a correctly weighted nymph which will sink fast and deep on a low-diameter nylon leader which is as fine as you dare go, and the use of polarizing glasses and an eye-shade to keep light from your eyes and to enable you to see through the surface and spot the fish.

12

RIVER TROUT

One of the greatest of fly-fishing pleasures is to be on the banks of a favourite trout-stream during the first flush of summer. It is a magical time, when the pale, bright green of new leaves gives a wonderful freshness to the scene, in stark contrast to the bleakness of winter. It is a pleasure reinforced by the sight of widening rings caused by a trout feeding confidently on a hatch of olive duns, picking off individual flies as they drift downstream.

Rivers which have the cool, well-oxygenated water needed to support trout can be broken down into two main types. The most numerous are the rain-fed or free-stone rivers which are fed literally by rain falling within a catchment area such as a range of hills. Rain-fed rivers vary from small streams or brooks that can be leapt across to great sprawling courses which power across the landscape through forests and rocky gorges. Their size varies dramatically, depending on conditions. Rain or melting snow flows quickly into the river's course, swelling it into a flood and adding colour in the form of suspended mud or silt. Conversely, in periods of dry weather the river's flow can be drastically reduced. Both scenarios can adversely effect the fishing.

ABOVE Catch-and-release is an important part of river trout fishing. Maintaining a healthy head of trout by limiting the kill allows the fish to grow large and also to sustain a viable population without recourse to restocking. Returning a trout should be done as quickly as possible after capture. Hands should be wet before the fish is touched to prevent its protective mucous being damaged. The fish should then be held facing upstream in clear, well-oxygenated water until its strength returns. The fish is ready to go when it makes strong thrusts of its tail.

LEFT Fishing small streams can be great fun. The fish may not be big, but they are often willing takers of a dry fly, though not necessarily a pushover. A careful approach is still required.

Sparkle Dun

Dry Hare's Ear

Thorax Danica Dun

Griffith's Sparkle Gnat

Petitjean Dun

Iron Blue

Beatis Spinner

Emerging Ephemerid

Troth Pheasant Tail

Cross-hackle Gnat

Amber Caddis Pupa

Although rain-fed rivers support a good population of both fish and invertebrate life, they are not rich. The bottom is often rocky and weed-growth is limited. Fish do grow to a good size, but to do so they must be opportunist feeders, taking a wide variety of prey, including terrestrial insects and aquatic insects such as upwinged flies, caddis-flies and stoneflies, and even small fish. But their wide-ranging tastes do not make these trout easy to catch, especially when a river is running low and clear. Tactics then need to be as refined and well controlled as on any other type of water.

LEFT A fine River Wharfe brown trout in the net. When small flies and light tippets are used, netting fish is often safer than bringing them to hand. Removing small patterns can be difficult, even with barbless hooks, and trying to control a good-sized fish on a light tippet can easily lead to a broken line. Netting the fish first with a net of soft, knotless mesh allows it to be handled confidently and the hook removed before it is returned.

BELOW Working a team of small wet flies or nymphs is a great way of tempting trout in rain-fed rivers. The technique is to cast the line slightly across the stream, letting the flies work round in the current. It works best when the river is at moderate height with a steady, but not excessive, flow rate. A middle-actioned rod is often used for this method, softer than would be needed for upstream dry fly.

132

The second type of river is the chalkstream. Often regarded as the archetypal trout habitat, chalkstreams offer a rich, lush environment which grows large, wily trout. Their richness comes from the geology of the surrounding land. Chalkstreams obtain the bulk of their flow from water which has seeped into underground aquifers through porous limestone, or chalk. This water eventually wells up in clear springs and the calcium, nitrates and carbon dioxide which have been dissolved in it make it alkaline and nutrient rich.

Because rain-water can take literally months to filter through the rock and into the river, this type of water is also very stable in both flow-rate and temperature, allowing plant and animal life to flourish. In even the warmest conditions, chalkstream water seldom exceeds 12 degrees centigrade, well within the 7–19 degree temperature range in which trout thrive.

For many anglers the cream of river trout fishing comes from imitative fly-fishing. This entails drifting

ABOVE Trout in the clear, shallow chalkstreams are wary of unnatural movement on their horizon. This angler breaks up his outline by concealing himself behind bankside vegetation. Keeping a low profile is especially important when approaching surface-feeding fish.

INSERT Parachute Grey Duster. This is a Parachute version of a traditional dry-fly pattern. Tied in this way, it makes a superb imitation of an emerging aquatic insect from an upwing to a small caddis-fly.

RIGHT On small rocky streams, such as Devon's East Lyn, trout can be picked off with both dry fly and nymph from small pockets, riffles and from behind large boulders. The brown trout here are not big, and a fish weighing more than 1lb is a relative giant. However, on a light brook rod rated for a weight 4 line, these beautiful wild fish can provide some fascinating high-summer fly-fishing.

ABOVE The mayfly hatch is a time of plenty for fish and angler alike. However, after a week or two of hard feeding, trout can become very selective. Patterns not only have to look right and be presented correctly, but they also have to feel right. Large, stiffly hackled flies, especially when tied on longshank hooks, are often rejected. Detached-body flies, such as the cutwing mayfly this fish has taken, are much more effective. They not only offer a more lifelike profile, but they also collapse easily when the fish takes and are not merely 'bumped' away. This 'suckability' is a prime factor when trying to fool wary trout with big dry flies.

LEFT On a number of rain-fed rivers throughout northern England and Scotland, but especially in Wales, late March to early April is the time for the March brown *Rhithrogena germanica*. Although the weather at this time of year can be horribly cold, this large, dark brownish dun, with heavily veined wings, hatches in sizable flurries during the middle part of the day when temperatures are at their highest. Although the rise may be sporadic, hatches of March brown produce wonderful early-season dry-fly fishing.

a small dry fly or nymph right into the path of a feeding trout, and it is the anticipation and then the immediacy of the action when the fly is sipped from the surface that makes it the most enthralling fishing of all. A large part of any river trout's diet is taken subsurface, when aquatic flies are hatching at the surface, the trout pick them off as they drift downstream.

A number of different aquatic and terrestrial insects are eaten by trout, but upwinged flies, of the Order Ephemeroptera, have the greatest influence on the river angler; indeed, many of the traditional dry-fly patterns are imitations of this group. Throughout the spring and summer months a wide range of ephemeropterans hatch in numbers large enough to trigger a substantial rise. The numbers of any one species can be so great that at times the fish will take them to the exclusion of all else. This preoccupation is the reason why precise imitation can be so crucial.

The predominant species early in the season, the large dark olive, *Baetis rhodani*, is most likely to be hatching during the cold, blustery days of April. Later, as the warmth of early summer brings insect and plant-life to a peak, other upwinged flies such as the medium olive, pale watery and small, dark iron blue, all members of the genus *Baetidae*, are taken in large numbers, in both the dun and spinner stages and as nymphs.

Late May and early June is a prime period on most rivers. It is also when Britain's largest ephemerid, the mayfly, *Ephemera danica*, hatches in prodigious numbers. It has a relatively short season, on some rivers as little as two weeks, though when the large, yellowish duns are on the water, it may seem that every trout and grayling in the river is feeding at the surface. Even birds cash in on this time of plenty, with everything from swallows and martins to the humble sparrow intercepting the duns as they make for cover.

Although the Shadow Mayfly looks very little like a real mayfly, its abstract qualities can fool the wiliest of trout. The body, heavily palmered with grizzle cock hackles, keeps the fly floating superbly.

After the abundance of the mayfly hatch, late June can be an anticlimax, though, as the trout settle into a more regular feeding pattern, smaller ephemerids, including the various *Baetis* species, plus the blue-winged olive *Ephemerella ignita*, become the most important to imitate. For many anglers, this is when true fly-fishing begins.

Caddis-flies, too, are an important food source on both chalkstreams and rain-fed rivers, particularly the latter. Though trout feed on the larvae and pupae throughout the day, it is late evening and into dark when the adults are taken in quantity. This is especially so during the heat of summer, when trout stay deep within the ranunculus and starwort weed-beds, feeding at the surface only after dusk when conditions are cooler.

A trout feeding steadily takes up a specific lie, and with stealth and the use of a pair of polarizing glasses to cut out surface glare, you can spend many fruitful and enjoyable moments watching how a fish reacts to a natural insect drifting into its field of view. Although it is nigh-on impossible to see the actual insect, if it is sub-surface, the demeanour of the trout, the way it becomes more alert, the way it sidles across stream, and the flash of white as its mouth opens and closes are all clues to its particular feeding pattern. Time

Bubble-back Emerging Ephemerid. A loop of *cul-de-canard* feather is tied to suggest the emerging wings and body of an ephemerid dun breaking free from its nymphal skin.

Summer evenings are the time of the spinner. When the air is still, great swarms of mating upwinged flies gather over the water in search of mates. Once the females have been fertilized, they return to the water to lay their eggs. This is accomplished, depending on the species, by dipping the abdomen in the water or by crawling beneath the surface and depositing eggs on submerged stones and weed. Once the spinner has completed this task, it dies, falling spent on the water. As this angler changes pattern, a cloud of *Baetis* spinners dances around him in the golden light.

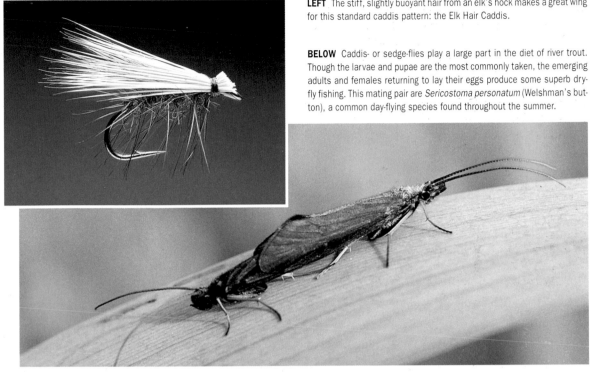

LEFT The stiff, slightly buoyant hair from an elk's hock makes a great wing for this standard caddis pattern: the Elk Hair Caddis.

BELOW Caddis- or sedge-flies play a large part in the diet of river trout. Though the larvae and pupae are the most commonly taken, the emerging adults and females returning to lay their eggs produce some superb dry-fly fishing. This mating pair are *Sericostoma personatum* (Welshman's button), a common day-flying species found throughout the summer.

spent like this, with the fly in the keeper ring, is never wasted. It provides a good lesson in water-craft, not least how to approach a fish without spooking it.

When a hatch of duns or a fall of spinners, or indeed almost any type of surface activity, is in full flow, a trout's feeding level is normally much closer to the surface. This obviously reduces the amount of effort needed to intercept any prey, but it also reduces the fish's field of view. So you have be really accurate in placing your fly where the fish can see it.

Trout have good all-round sight. Each eye has a 180-degree field of vision which overlaps at the front and above the head for about 30 degrees. This overlap provides the trout with frontal binocular vision which gives a large depth of field,

During a good hatch of duns, trout hang just under the surface, picking off individual insects as they drift into range. The rise-form is leisurely. The duns are drifting with the current, and all the trout has to do is to sip them in. This type of rise often leaves a single bubble, made as the trout takes in air at the surface. It is a good way of distinguishing this rise from one to emerging nymph, which never leaves a tell-tale bubble.

allowing it to see objects clearly even at range and to judge distance accurately.

The overlap also means that the fish's vision is poor or even non-existent in an equal 30-degree section at its rear. This blind spot can be exploited, allowing the fish to be approached from behind without it being able to see the angler. But trout have an upward angle of view of 97 degrees. This angle remains the same irrespective of the depth at which the trout is lying, so the closer to the surface the fish is, the smaller its window of sight. This means that when trout are finning just below the surface, a typical scenario is a steady stream of duns or spinners on the water, the cast has to be very accurate for the fish to see the imitation. The same applies when fish are feeding sub-surface except that without the surface to focus the fish at a particular level, it is more difficult to target them accurately.

An upstream approach is usually the most effective, especially when fish are feeding actively at or near the surface. Here the line is cast upstream of the angler, anywhere from almost at a right-angle to the flow to directly upstream. The exact angle depends on where the fish is rising in relation to the angler. For example, if the fish is lying exactly opposite, the cast is made at about 70 degrees to the flow and at a range so that the fly lands 3–6 feet upstream of that point. With fish cruising close to the surface, 1ft can be enough, but trout normally lie a few feet upstream of where the rise is seen. This needs to be compensated for when judging the amount of lead drift required.

One advantage of this method is that the angler remains downstream of the fish, outside or at the limit of its field of view; only the fly and a length of fine nylon leader pass over the fish. The other main advantage is that because the line is drifting towards the angler, it keeps the fly on a natural drift and deters the enemy of correct dry-fly presentation – drag. Drag occurs when the fly travels faster than the current, by the same principal that allows a water-skier, by cutting across the direction of pull, to go faster than the towing craft.

Watch a real insect drifting downstream and you can see that the only action upon it comes from the flow and any prevailing breeze. What the fly rarely does is

Drag on a dry fly or nymph can be combated by making one or more upstream mends with the fly-line. This is done with a flick of the rod-top, throwing a wave of line upstream and causing a length of slack line to form which must be straightened by the current before the fly drags. Multiple line mends are possible only with a floating line or a sink-tip, which has a floating belly.

suddenly plough across the surface, throwing up a small but definite bow wave. Unfortunately, unlike the real thing, imitations have a third force working upon them – the line. After a cast, the current quickly catches the thick fly-line, taking it off downstream and rapidly forming a belly in it. As soon as it straightens, any slack in the leader begins to pull the fly, causing it to skate unnaturally. You can be lucky. Occasionally that small acceleration induces a fish to grab hold. More often, the unnatural movement simply makes it reject the fly or, worse still, bolt in panic.

The remedy is to cast a snaky line, producing curves which the current must straighten for the line to drag. This gives the fly a vital few seconds of natural drift, uninterrupted except, hopefully, by the sip of a taking fish. The period of drag-free drift can be extended by a second ploy, that of making one or more upstream mends in the line as it is carried downstream. A 'mend' is simply a small wave of line thrown upstream with a flick of the rod-tip. It puts extra slack in the line, increasing the time before it draws tight; however, this

is possible only with a floating line as this can easily be picked off the surface.

Drag is especially a problem when you are fishing at long range and when the water is moving quickly. The more line you cast, the more line the current has to act upon. Even on relatively short casts, as soon as the fly has begun its drift, the fly-line is retrieved. The speed at which this happens depends on the river's flow rate. The line should be picked off the water as soon as any belly forms, for once it gets downstream of the angler, retrieving it is almost impossible without altering the drift of the fly. A belly also has to be lifted from the water and straightened before a fish can be struck. The greater the belly, the more difficult, if not impossible, this becomes.

To combat this, approach as close to the fish as possible, so that the length of line on the water is controllable. This often entails wading, which in most situations, and done carefully, is a great way of positioning yourself to achieve the right presentation. In shallow water thigh-waders are adequate, but in deeper water chest-waders may be necessary. Keep all movements slow and

137

Where bankside vegetation restricts the back-cast, wading is sometimes the only method of covering a difficult lie. Although thigh-waders are adequate, neoprene chest-waders are not only warmer, but they allow the angler to reach spots which would otherwise be unfishable. Care should be taken in deep wading, not only to avoid slipping, but also to prevent any weed-beds from being destroyed. If the river is particularly deep or powerful, the wearing of an automatically inflated life-jacket is advised: it could save your life.

deliberate and it should be possible to approach within 10yd of a feeding fish; close enough to achieve a really accurate presentation. Wading can be a real advantage even on small rivers; indeed where a stream is overgrown or fringed with trees and other tall vegetation, wading can offer the only chance of a clear back-cast.

But wading is not always possible. Deep water and no-wading rules in force on some waters mean that heavy mending and basic line control are necessary skills for the river fly-fisher to master. It is all to do with presentation, for whether you are fishing upstream or down, the ability to control the fly's path, to make it do want you want, is always going to be far more effective than chuck-it-and-chance-it.

Drag isn't such a great problem in nymph fishing as it is when dry fly is being used; nevertheless, the fact that drag results in a loss of control means that it should be eliminated whenever possible even when you are fishing sub-surface patterns. When fishing a nymph upstream the method for eradicating drag is the same as for dry-fly fishing. By mending the line so that the fly moves at the same speed as the current, it can be

LEFT The Adams is a general upwing pattern which has proved deadly the world over. Mixing the grizzle and red game hackles as a collar gives the fly a superb 'buzz'.

BELOW So long as the reel has a good, even drag mechanism which gives as a fish bolts, even very big trout can be landed on tiny flies and ultra-light tippets. This plump chalkstream brown trout was feeding on a hatch of medium olive and was fooled by a size 18 Adams.

138

fished effectively in a style known as dead-drift. Dead-drift is simply that the fly is allowed to drift with the current without movement induced by the angler. It is effective because not only does it allow the nymph to sink readily to the fish's level, but it allows it to move in a lifelike manner. Small invertebrates which have been disturbed often ride the current with hardly a twitch before falling to the bottom or hitting a weed-bed. They don't swing in a great arc across the current. Heavy fishing pressure and catch-and-release pro-duces fish which are wary of poor or unnatural presen-tation, and even when the pattern looks lifelike, if it doesn't drift like the real thing it is studiously ignored.

An adaption of this is the fly-first principle. It was developed to allow fishing at range to ultra-cautious trout which had become used to a fly presented upstream. This is a particular problem on clear, shal-low streams, where the sight of a fly-line drifting by can spook even deep-lying trout. Although the fly is

presented downstream to the fish, before it sees either leader or fly line, the method should not be confused with standard downstream wet-fly and nymph tactics. With fly-first, the object is to put plenty of line on to the water to provide the weight to allow further line to be paid out and carried on the current without affect-ing the drift of the fly.

A floating line is used to fish a nymph in this fashion, and the pattern is usually well weighted. If the water is deep, in excess of 8–10ft, or the current powerful, a sinking braided leader is also employed to take the fly quickly to the bottom. The line is cast high so that instead of the leader turning over, the fly lands as close to the tip of the line as possible. This means that fly and leader can sink without being immediately pulled by the fly-line as it is grabbed by the current. The fly-line is also cast either at right-angles to the flow or slightly downstream, so that the fly and leader land exactly on the line you wish them to travel down. This can be a path

On the slower, deeper stretches of a river, where the surface is glassy smooth, fine lines and small flies often form the only really successful tactic. The calm water and relatively slow drift of the fly gives the fish plenty of time to examine an imitation. Scaling down to a leader as fine as 1½– 2lb breaking-strain is often necessary, particularly when the fly used is in the 18–24 range. Difficult fish such as this are prime targets for the fly- first approach, though on waters such as the River Kennet, pictured here, the rule is upstream only.

either through a weed-bed or where the river bottom drops away; places where trout are likely to be lying.

As the fly-line begins to move with the current, more line should be fed out by wiggling the rod-top, so that at no time does the line draw tight, which would cause the fly to lift out of position. The only exception to this is a brief pause to make the fly rise a few inches, rather as it would in a standard induced take. The result is often much the same, a fish grabbing a fly which seemed about to escape.

Takes are detected at short to medium range by a pause or dip in the end of the fly-line. At longer distances, in excess of 15yd, a sight-bob is necessary if many takes are not to be missed. Sight-bobs, or bite-indicators, are made either from a buoyant plastic foam or from polypropylene yarn which also floats well. Whatever the material, most come in high-visibility, fluorescent colours such as orange, red or yellow. These bobs allow a pause, dip or stab of the line to be seen easily, even in a riffle.

Fly-first is also applicable to dry-fly fishing, and for the same reasons. Ultra-cautious fish which might spook at the sight of a fly-line flashing nearby can be fooled if the fly is allowed to drift down into their path from long range. Once the target fish has been sighted, and its feeding pattern identified, the line is cast slightly downstream of the angler so that the leader lands with a snaky profile with the fly on the same line but well upstream of the fish. The rod-top is then wiggled from side to side to pay out fly-line until the fly reaches the fish. Don't strike immediately when a fish takes; let the fish drop back to its feeding level, or at least to close its mouth first. If you don't, what happens is that your fly comes back quicker than you expected and the fish is

put down. Solving the problem of just where to put the fly in the first place takes experience. You need to be able to judge accurately exactly where the fly is going to be once it has drifted 10 or even 20yd downstream. It is a technique which should be well practised on a stretch of river where mistakes don't matter.

This fly-first technique has a further advantage in that it allows fish to be covered in large, wide pools, where distance and the angler's inability to wade means they cannot be approached with standard upstream tactics. The angler may be able to wade in at the neck of the pool and fish down imitatively to rising

One way of landing a trout is to dispense with a landing net entirely and bring it to hand. It is a method which works best where an area of slack water is nearby into which the fish can be guided. Here, in what is obviously a fast-moving river, this angler is in danger of losing a beautifully conditioned rainbow trout. The twists and turns of a fish of this size at such close quarters can easily snap a light leader. However, the fish will be returned in any case, so the loss of a fly is no great hardship.

or deep-lying fish 20 or 30yd away, even where the water is swift and broken. Beware though, some waters have upstream-only restrictions. Check the rules first!

Tackle for river trout fishing varies depending on the size of the water. On a small overgrown brook, a 6ft rod rated for a 3–4 weight line is perfect; short enough to be threaded through bankside vegetation and capable of handling the small flies and light tippets necessary for wild and wary fish. As with all types of river fly-fishing, braided tapered leaders or steeply tapering nylon leaders help to transmit the power of the cast through to the fly, helping it to turn over properly.

On medium-sized waters, which include even the widest, most powerful chalkstreams, most techniques such as dry fly and standard weighted nymph can be tackled with a 7½–8½ft rod rated for a number 5 line. A rod of this build, with a middle-to-tip action, is both light and accurate enough to place a dry fly within inches of a likely looking spot, as well as allowing casts of 20yd or more with little difficulty. It is also able to handle leaders as light as 2lb breaking-strain and flies as small as size 20, or even smaller without the constant threat of tearing them from the fish's mouth.

On the largest rivers, which are still fishable with a fly, a 9½ft rod rated for a number 6 line is capable of punching flies as large as a dry mayfly into a stiff downstream breeze. It is also capable of handling the big, heavily weighted nymphs and braided leaders so effective in deep water and in fast-flowing, rain-fed rivers.

The obvious giveaway of river trout is the rise – from where a fish breaks surface. The fact that the water is flowing is also a help, as fish invariably lie facing upstream. However, when trout are feeding sub-surface, with no obvious indication as to their whereabouts, an understanding of what makes a good trout lie is a great advantage. Any river has specific areas which hold fish

141

During early summer, when beds of *Ranunculus* wave thick and green in the crystal water of a chalkstream, trout hang in the open channels between them, picking off small invertebrates such as *Gammarus* and various aquatic insect larvae. An artificial nymph should be allowed to dead-drift through these channels. This is achieved by casting upstream and allowing the fly to drift back with the current.

142

and others which are either devoid or which support only the smaller trout. Brown trout, particularly, are territorial and the larger fish are often found in the best-protected spots or areas with a natural food trap or channel.

CDC Dun. Tied in a range of sizes and body shades, this pattern can be used to imitate any of the smaller upwinged species.

Smaller, less-dominant fish have to make do with less productive spots, to the extent that if they do stray into another fish's territory, they are quickly chased off.

Trout like areas which make them feel safe, so bridges, weed-beds, overhanging trees and even submerged fence posts, which all afford a degree of cover, are likely spots. When trout are feeding on nymphs, channels in weed-beds are a particular favourite. Here fish can hover along the edge of the weed, sidling across current to pick up any small creature drifting down. Beneath an overhanging tree is also a good spot, although presenting a fly through a tangle of branches may be a problem. Not only do low branches make good cover for trout, but trees contain large populations of beetles, bugs and small caterpillars, and all are only one small slip from a watery grave.

Effective dry-fly patterns include dun imitations such as the CDC Dun, the Sparkle Dun and the Adams. The Adams, with its grey body, grizzle hackle-tips and mixed grizzle and red game hackle is a general suggestion of an upwinged fly and is deadly throughout the season.

FACTFILE

For most river situations a rod 8½–9ft in length rated for an AFTM 5–6 line will seldom be found wanting. It is long enough to cover most techniques, from dry fly to heavy nymph, and is also delicate enough to handle delicate tippets as light as 1½lb breaking strain that are required to fish size 20–24 nymphs and dry flies effectively.

Though a double taper or weight forward floating line is the standard river approach, other line densities, from intermediate to fast sinking, can be used if water conditions dictate. Sinking, tapered braided leaders may also be used; these allow even quite small, light patterns to be fished close to the bottom in fast, powerful or very deep water.

When fly fishing on rivers, the range of casts required is also greater than on stillwater. Though distance isn't usually a problem, odd currents, overhanging bushes and restricted back

casts make it imperative that a wide range of techniques, from the roll cast, side cast and reach cast, are needed to place that fly accurately where a fish is lying.

When dry-fly fishing, apart from notable exceptions such as skating an adult caddis imitation, the fly should always drift with the current. While the same applies to most types of nymph fishing, there are tricks to make otherwise wily fish take. One such ploy is the induced take. Here the nymph is allowed to drift downstream while the rod is kept low; then as the nymph approaches the fish at the correct depth the rod is raised. This has the effect of making the nymph rise in the water and accelerate just as if it were trying to escape; the trout responds by grabbing it. It is a technique which relies upon the predatory instincts of the trout and is often exceedingly effective.

 # GRAYLING

Grayling are found throughout large parts of southern and northern Europe, Canada and Siberia, where they favour cool, clear, well-oxygenated water. Although the ranges of the two species overlap, *Thymallus thymallus* and *Thymallus arcticus* are generally found in different regions. Of the two, *T. arcticus* has the more northerly distribution and is often called the Arctic grayling. The European grayling extends to more southerly climes, well into southern Europe where it inhabits water types similar to those favoured by brown trout, though it is less tolerant of poor water quality than the trout.

Though it thrives in a range of water types, including chalkstreams, freestone or rain-fed rivers make an ideal habitat; from tumbling, gravelly streams to great rocky rivers. Of the two, it is generally the larger rivers which produce the largest grayling, specimens of

which can exceed 4½lb. That said, a 2lb-plus grayling is a big fish. The average is a good deal less.

The use of leaded, fast-sinking nymphs and bugs is an effective technique for catching grayling. It also provides a perfect example of the effectiveness of correct presentation. Sub-surface flies are all too often skimmed over a fish's head rather than being allowed to sink to the holding level. Although grayling do feed at the surface, particularly when a hatch of fly is on, much of their feeding is nearer the river-bed. This is especially true during cold weather, when surface-feeding is at best sporadic and at worst non-existent.

The grayling's down-turned mouth is a clear indication of its preferred feeding habits. Crustaceans such as the freshwater shrimp (*Gammarus* spp.), caddis larvae and the nymphs of stoneflies and upwinged flies make

up the bulk of its diet. These creatures inhabit the bottom layers of the river, amongst gravel or clinging to water-smoothed rocks; or the middle layers, living concealed among weed-fronds. These are important clues in creating and fishing grayling patterns effectively.

Whether it is when they are dislodged by grayling looking for food, or when they are migrating to another part of the river or ascending to the surface before emerging as adults, these small invertebrates tend to be snapped up within inches of the river-bed. It makes sense to present the fly at this depth, at the level at which grayling are most likely to be feeding.

Early afternoon is the grayling's prime feeding time during the cooler, shortening days of autumn. This is when the sun is at its height, and temperatures, although low, are at their greatest. In the cold, well-oxygenated water the fish keep to pools and deeper, smoother glides, forsaking the more broken water. This is a particularly good-looking spot; a smooth glassy glide which seems to shout 'grayling'!

The commonest methods of fishing weighted patterns are the down-and-across and upstream nymph styles. In the former, the line is cast at an angle of about 70–45 degrees

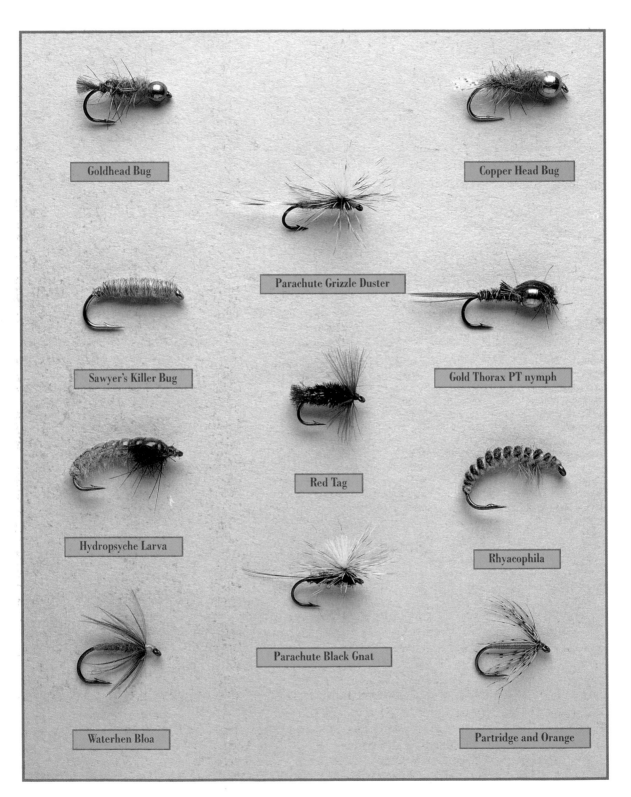

Goldhead Bug

Copper Head Bug

Parachute Grizzle Duster

Sawyer's Killer Bug

Gold Thorax PT nymph

Hydropsyche Larva

Red Tag

Rhyacophila

Parachute Black Gnat

Waterhen Bloa

Partridge and Orange

ABOVE A short across-stream cast, no more than 10yd, and the fly will work back nicely with the current. A heavy fly should be cast on an open loop to avoid clipping the rod-top, and the casting action should be slowed down to accommodate the drag of the heavy fly on the line. The fly lands with a gentle 'plop' and a quick, downstream mend of the line ensures that the nymph continues to sink on a dead-drift along the edge of the weed-bed. Keeping the fly drifting directly downstream on a slack line ensures that it doesn't swing off-line and hang up on weed.

RIGHT The first run down produces nothing. A slightly longer cast is made with an open loop kicked high to keep disturbance to a minimum. Again the line is mended almost immediately downstream, the fly working nice-ly with the current so that it bumps seductively along the bottom; exactly where feeding grayling might be holding station. The tip of the line is almost directly opposite when it twitches sharply. A swift lift of the rod meets the firm resistance of a very good fish.

downstream across the flow and the flies allowed to swing round with the current. The angle depends on the speed of the river; the faster the water, the larger the angle, giving the fly time to sink to the fish's depth before the current lifts the line and pulls the fly off the bottom. A short downstream mend in the line helps the flies sink. Two or three yards of fly-line are flipped quickly downstream just after the cast and before the current has a chance to grab hold, which keeps the flies drifting on a slack line for longer and increases their sinking time.

In thin water, 1½–2ft deep, two useful patterns are a size 14 or 16 Pheasant Tail Nymph or Hare's Ear Nymph, both carrying a small amount of extra weight. In normal depths, 2–4ft, a heavier pattern is neces-sary, and a Leaded Shrimp, or a sombre-coloured bug with a gold or copper head should catch fish.

In a strong current, the large, pronounced dorsal fin of a grayling whips the fish off downstream. Control is achieved by keeping the rod high to clear any weed before dropping the rod to give side-strain as the fish reaches more open water. Keeping the rod low prevents the grayling hitting the surface and thrashing about. After a few tense minutes, the fish finally turns on its flanks, ready for netting.

Grayling are obliging fish, and provided you remain still, it is possible to watch a shoal at close quarters in clear, shallow water. One of the most useful lessons comes from watching how the various fish in the shoal react to fly patterns. The first time grayling see a pattern such as a Goldhead, the effect can be dramatic; even quite large fish barge through the shoal to grab it. But, after a few drifts down, the response changes dramatically; fish either refuse or even shy away as the Goldhead bumps past them. Toning down to a more sombre, or more imitative, pattern is almost always the solution.

In deeper water, or when the river is clearing after a spate, larger, heavier patterns come into their own. Cased caddis imitations such as the

ABOVE A moment is spent admiring the blues and oranges of the sail-like dorsal fin, contrasting with the grey-flushed lilac of the grayling's flanks. Held into the current, the fish soon regains its strength. Grayling often fight to exhaustion, and cradling a played-out specimen, head into the flow, pushes oxygenated water through the gills and quickly revives it before a kick of its tail sends it gliding off into the dark water.

RIGHT After the give-and-take of the line customary with a large grayling in peak condition, the net is brought into position as the fish tires. Seconds later it is enveloped within the meshes of the net and the hook is removed. With a fine line and a strong current, netting makes the fish easier to deal with, preventing any last minute snap-offs as it twists and turns on a short line.

Peeping Caddis and the Grub Head Caddis are effective even when tied on size 8 longshank hooks. Their size and weight is no deterrent to the grayling, and allow better fly-control when the river is powering through.

Takes appear either as a steady tightening of the line or as a definite pull. Either way, the fish is usually hooked by the bow in the line. And although the angler is trying to keep the fly at the grayling's depth, the final lift, as the current acts on the line, often induces a fish into taking as the fly rises and accelerates away.

A team of light spider patterns is effective when grayling are feeding nearer the surface, using the down-and-across style, with the tiny, sparsely dressed flies worked through the pools and runs on a

Although grayling shoals normally contain fish of mixed sizes, it pays to move if numbers of small 'nursery' grayling are found. Areas containing these fish rarely hold better specimens. Conversely, the largest grayling tend to be more solitary in habit, appearing in places which don't normally produce large numbers of fish. In clear, shallow water it is possible to spot grayling feeding on small invertebrates, drifting to and fro across the stream and intercepting small prey items as they come down on the current.

Fishing down-and-across the stream can be effective in stretches of river with a steady, medium-paced flow. Here a team of small spider patterns is cast at an angle and allowed to swing gently round in the current. If the water is moving quickly, causing the flies to skate, a downstream mend made just after the cast throws a length of slack into the line, giving the flies longer to sink before they start to swing and lift.

The water is about 3ft deep, so teaming an AFTM 5 floating line with a 9ft long leader of 3lb breaking-strain nylon is a perfect starting point. A mid-range cast – 10–15yd – is more than adequate to cover the water, and an 8–9ft rod capable of throwing a five-weight line makes an effective but delicate tool. In this part of the river, where the surface is smooth and unruffled, grayling quickly respond even to a small insect hatch. A similar-sized dry fly such as a Hare's Ear or a CDC dun, cast upstream, will pick off rising fish.

floating line. It is a deadly method on rain-fed rivers when fish are feeding on small baetid nymphs such as those of the iron blue and the small dark olive, or on tiny species of stonefly nymphs.

Upstream nymphing is an exceptionally good method when the fish will take the nymph only when it is dead-drifted with no hint of swing. The line is cast either directly upstream or at a slight angle across and the fly drifted back on a slack line. Fished in this way, the nymph, usually well weighted, can be allowed to tumble along close to the river bed in a manner similar to that of a small invertebrate which has been disturbed and is drifting free with the current. Most small to medium-sized weighted patterns work with this technique, from a simple grey Sawyer's Bug, to a Leaded Shrimp, Rhyacophila Larva or a Goldhead Bug.

Signs of a take when the upstream nymph is being fished vary from the merest pause of the leader to a sharp jab as the grayling picks up the nymph and swings across the current. At short range, 5–10yd, watching the leader is easy. At longer range, or in more broken water, a high-visibility indicator is a positive advantage. A small section of brightly coloured foam, slipped over the leader, or a short length of wool inserted through the braid, are both good methods. Here Charles Jardine uses the sight-bob method on Austria's River Traun.

A derivation of the basic upstream nymph tactic is a method known as the rolled nymph. It is a technique which can be accomplished properly only by deep wading, so chest-waders are a must. Its success owes much to the fact that grayling are extremely tolerant fish. Long casting is not needed; indeed, for much of the time only a few feet of fly-line are outside the tip-ring. The technique involves casting a heavily weighted nymph slightly upstream and allowing it, by following its path with the rod-top, to bump along the bottom for a few yards. Because so little line is used, the nymph's drift is never impeded and because it doesn't swing, it can be fished even through narrow channels in the weed-beds – exactly where many grayling feed.

To keep drag to a minimum, the rod is held high, with as much line as possible off the water. Takes are signalled either by a draw on the line or a pause in its natural speed of drift. The response should be a firm tightening, though with so short a line a vicious strike must be avoided. Takes are easy to spot at this close range, though it is easy to mistake them for the fly catching bottom. If takes aren't forthcoming after a few runs down, step downstream and repeat the process. In this way a good length of river can be covered and lies with feeding grayling located.

Because the drift is so short, patterns for the rolled nymph method need to be heavy and quick-sinking. As caddis larva figure highly in the grayling's diet, imitations such as the Hydropsyche Larva are deadly, as are some of the larger gold and copper bead flies, especially those with a lead underbody.

Though nymph tactics are probably the most effective, a well-presented dry fly produces some wonderful sport at times. A weak glimmer of sunshine and a small hatch of upwinged flies or midges will bring grayling to the top even in the depths of winter, and even an insignificant looking-rise form, the merest dimple on a glassy surface, may be a large grayling on the feed. Small flies and fine lines are the key in such conditions, especially if frosts and lack of rain see the river running low and clear.

During autumn and summer with good fly hatches throughout the day, grayling often take a dry fly in the same region as trout. The rise-form is usually much less showy than the trout's, even when the same type of insect is being taken; but it is no less deliberate. For most of the time these insects, usually the duns of various upwing species, are relatively small and their imitations easily taken by the grayling. However, when larger insects are the fare, such as the mayfly, *Ephemera danica*, hooking grayling can be problem. It is not that they won't take an artificial; rather is it that imitations are too stiff and unyielding. The grayling's gentle approach and small mouth mean that big patterns fished right

Keeping the rod high as the fly ends its run is the basic 'high-stick' tactic with the rolled nymph. Heavy, quick-sinking patterns such as Goldheads are great for searching the water; the flash of gold is an attractor to feeding grayling. However, quick success is often transitory, for in clear water the fish soon become used to this gaudy type of fly. However, the main aim has been achieved – a shoal has been located. Working more sombre patterns, both general or more specific imitations, usually winkles out more and bigger fish.

The F Fly, devised by Marjan Fratnick, is a wonderfully simple pattern using a wing of cul-de-canard feather to deadly effect.

on the surface are literally pushed away. The problem can be solved by using a detached-body pattern which folds up as the fish sucks it down.

With dry flies, grayling have a real preference for patterns which sit right in the surface film. Anything which sits high on steely hackle-fibres certainly attracts fish, but results in too many abortive offers. Small Parachute-hackled flies are extremely effective, patterns such as the Grey Duster and the Gulper tied on size 14 to 20 light wire hooks. So, too, are flies which use *cul-de-canard* feathers as a wing or hackle. They sit low, just at the right level, and the softness of the hackle makes them easy for the grayling to sip off the surface. Patterns range from simple affairs such as the original F fly devised by Marian Fratnick to a CDC Thorax Dun designed to imitate species including the

Small emerger-type patterns are particularly effective for the surface-feeding grayling, often far better than high-riding dry flies. This well-conditioned autumn fish fell for a size 16 Hare's Ear.

The Klinkhammer Special was developed by Hans Van Klinken of the Netherlands. Though tied on a size 8–14 curved shank hook, the large size doesn't seem to deter the grayling.

large dark olive, *Baetis rhodani* and the medium olive, *Baetis vernus*. In smooth glides, even flies with no hackle at all are deadly. A small dry Hare's Ear tied in sizes 16–20, with a few fibres picked out at the thorax to help it float, is a superb flat-water pattern.

The same low-profile fly preference occurs in more broken water, too, but patterns may be a good deal larger. The most obvious example is the Klinkhammer Spe-

151

In fast or heavy broken water the sink-rate of a nymph can be helped by using a specially constructed sinking leader. This type of leader has lead or copper wire wound through its braided length, allowing the fly to be controlled more easily and fished at the correct depth. This method is often more effective than using a full sinking line, as a floating fly-line can be mended to alter the rate of swing and watched for signs of the take.

cial, devised by Dutch fly-tier Hans Van Klinken. Again, it is a Parachute-style tying using a modified curved shank emerger hook for the body and thorax. Although this is novel in itself, what is exceptional is the size. The overall length of the Klinkhammer is as much as ¾in, far larger than is generally accepted as a grayling fly. This matters little. The position the fly holds in the surface seems to be the key, and by slightly bending the front portion of an emerger hook before tying, the wing can be made to hold the abdomen almost directly downward. Van Klinken's rationale for this is that it imitates a hatching caddis-fly, but whatever the reason, it is a very effective pattern for broken or riffled water.

More traditional types of dry fly are also effective in riffles, particularly small palmered dressings in which the extra turns of hackle help support the fly, preventing water turbulence swamping it. Griffith's Gnat, Grizzle Palmer and Elkhair Caddis all work well, especially the latter, which bobs along like a cork on broken water. However, all these palmered flies should have the hackle trimmed short beneath the hook so that they sit low in the water, thereby reducing the number of abortive rises.

FACTFILE

The rod used is 8–9ft long and has a middle-to-tip action which is quick enough to cast even heavily weighted flies accurately. This is important when attempting to fish flies on a perfect downstream drift between weed channels.

A single-action lightweight reel rated for a 5/6 line is light enough for the rod, but has ample capacity for both fly line and 100yd of backing. The adjustable disc drag is sensitive enough for use with fine leaders, even in fast water.

The fly line is an AFTM 5 or 6 with a weight-forward profile. This is an advantage for increased distance, but more importantly, in this instance, because it loads the rod quickly to assist short, accurate casting with a heavy fly. A high-visibility yellow or orange indicator is perfect for showing takes.

The leader is in two parts. For general nymph fishing, the first section, connected to the fly-line itself, is 9ft of tapered, braided nylon with an intermediate sink-rate. This is ample for fishing in depths of 2–4ft, and the progressive taper of the braided leather transfers the power of the cast right through to the fly, helping casting. The conspicuous braid is connected to the fly with 3ft of 3–5lb breaking-strain nylon. This combination gives the advantage of good presentation with the delicacy of fine monofilament nylon. For faster or deeper water, higher densities of braided leather can be used. Those which have copper or lead wire running through them sink rapidly, taking the fly to the grayling's depth quickly and efficiently. For dry-fly work a tapered nylon leader can be used, or a floating braided leader with a 3ft tippet of light nylon monofilament.

The flies used include various coloured Goldhead bugs, Sawyer's Killer Bug and Hare's Ear Bug for initial 'water-searching', and the Freshwater Shrimp, Rhyacophila Larva and Hydropsyche Larva to fool more wily specimen grayling. Goldheads come in a wide range of sizes and colours, and although they may be used to suggest caddis pupae, larvae and shrimps, their main advantage is that they sink quickly. Even heavier patterns, such as the Peeping Caddis and the Grub Head Caddis work well in deeper or fast water.

A small Pheasant Tail or Hare's Ear Nymph in sizes 14–16 is deadly for fishing nearer the surface. On rain-fed streams spider patterns such as the Snipe and Purple, Partridge and Orange, Waterhen Bloa and Dark Needle are effective fished down-and-across.

Small imitative dry flies such as the Cul-de-canard F fly or the CDC dun work well in sizes 14–20, as do Hare's Ear or a Grey or Grizzle Duster tied Parachute-style.

14 CATCH-AND-RELEASE

The issue of catch-and-release trout-fishing becomes more and more a talking point among serious fly-fishers. Catch-and-release has slowly crept up on us, mainly over the last five years, and without pressure being put on fly-fishers, it has become the 'in-thing' to slip the occasional trout or two back with no fuss.

But the subject is controversial and emotive with both fishermen and fishery owners. Many anglers feel that if they pay a high price for a day-ticket, they are entitled to their 'pound of flesh'. A limit-bag is always at the back of their minds – 'limititis' it was dubbed by

Many experienced fly-fishers who fish for brown trout don't bother to use a landing-net, because they return their fish. The chance that one may escape before being brought to hand doesn't bother them. Here Peter admires a good brown and poses for a photograph, but normally he would slip the hook out with the fish still in the water.

one well-known angler some years ago. The signs are, however, that the ailment from which most anglers used to suffer, ourselves included, is being replaced by a more sporting outlook. The catching of fish is now, for many, thrill enough.

The turning point was perhaps in 1988, when the World Fly Fishing Championships were fished on the lakes of central Tasmania. England were defending their win of the previous year, when too-high a fish-kill had been made. This time, thanks to the United States, plans had been made for the competition to go ahead without any trout being killed. Competitors had to use barbless hooks and each one had a controller with him throughout the match. A hooked trout had to be brought to net and kept in the water at the bank side. The controller would then place the fish in a special measuring tray and record the length in centimetres. The de-barbed hook was easily slipped out and the fish returned quickly and little the worse for its experience.

These fish were strong and wild, and everything worked perfectly. In pre-competition practice the England party caught 180 trout, mostly browns but with some good rainbows. Only a few of these were killed for the stomach contents to be checked. In the event England retained the world crown with a massive points victory and not a dead fish in sight. With the world's top fly-fishers now officially practising catch-and-release, the message had to be spread.

Another type of fly-fisherman in Britain has always practised catch-and-release, the angler who fishes the wild lochs and rough streams. Catching lots of small wild browns rather than stocked rainbows, these anglers think nothing of returning perhaps 20 fish and keeping a brace of the best for the table. Such wild fish which are returned are none the worse because of their hardiness.

Conservation-minded fly-fishers who fish the big reservoirs are beginning to adopt the same approach. Hard-core regulars at most reservoirs certainly return all early-season brown trout, and a good number return all brown trout throughout the season, no matter what

A large brown is unhooked and quickly released, and no harm will come to it. Most catch-and-release enthusiasts compress the barb of their fly before beginning to fish.

A nice clean rainbow, but a little on the small side for Peter Cockwill, so he is returning it, keeping it over the water in case it should slip from his hand while it is unhooked. This is far better than taking fish on to the bank.

LEFT This rainbow has been netted, but the angler has kept the mesh containing the fish in the water. Then he has slipped the hook out and is about to send the fish on its way. This is an acceptable method.

the size or condition. The thinking is that browns live much longer than rainbows and that they are in the minority – perhaps one brown to every hundred rainbows in the stocking ratio. So, return a brown and catch an extra rainbow, which will eat better anyway.

Reservoir trout are very hardy. After being stocked at around 1lb, they soon toughen up and become fit, muscular specimens, putting on weight quickly. Fish which are returned seem perfectly happy and swim off at speed. It seems that, like the river and loch trout, they are none the worse for being hooked.

Catch-and-release can be practised in two ways. First, use a fly tied on a single barbless or de-barbed hook, play the fish firmly, but instead of drawing it to the net, bring it to hand. Then reach for the hook-bend and grip it tightly between finger and thumb. The trout should wriggle off the hook easily without leaving the water and without being touched.

The second method is to use a landing-net, but then to keep the trout in it in the water while it is unhooked. This is acceptable, but the first method is best for the fish.

Care is needed when fishing catch-and-release. Never net a fish and then bring it into the boat, where it may thrash about, bumping itself on the woodwork. Never hold a fish firmly while the hook is being taken out; and if the fly is in deeply, and if the fish is bleeding, kill it. Never beach a fish and allow it to flap about on dry soil, sand or gravel. Fish so treated stand little chance of surviving.

This brown is perfectly hooked in the scissors. Fish rarely come off when hooked in this position, but they are easy to unhook with a finger and thumb grip on the hook-shank.

International fly-fisher Brian Thomas caught this fine wild rainbow from a shallow Tasmanian lake. He beached the fish in inches of water before unhooking and returning it in an upright position.

Catch-and-release competitions have been held at small fisheries holding recently stocked and easily caught sizeable rainbows. Such fish are nowhere hardy enough to withstand catch-and-release, and Nigel Jackson, owner of the Dever Springs, has proved that fatalities follow the return of such fish. Fisheries which stock large rainbow trout should not allow catch-and-release at all. It is far better for anglers to keep to the permitted fishery limit.

One happy story about catch-and-release concerns grayling. Not everyone regards grayling as a true game-fish, and because they are not covered by the trout close season, trout fishers may continue to fish for them after trout fishing closes, with October and November prime fishing months.

Not a good way to hold a trout. The natural reaction is to squeeze tighter if the fish wriggles, and this can seriously damage it.

The cradling handhold is safer, and the fish will come to no harm.

ABOVE Brook trout are few and far between in the UK, and a quick release is the right thing.

ABOVE RIGHT Another good technique of bringing fish to hand is to keep it in the water while the fly-hook is slipped out.

RIGHT Little wild river browns should be placed back in the water with their heads facing upstream. They soon recover to take up their place in the stream.

Peter knows this is an exceptional brown. The question is, does he keep it, or does he put it back?

This brown has been netted and unhooked on the bank. This should be done only as a last resort, and it is not recommended.

FACTFILE

Some fisheries in Britain, usually the larger waters, do practise catch-and-release, and it is held to work. Small fishery owners, on the other hand, oppose it, probably with good reason. Fish caught and released in a small fishery have been seen to be distressed for days afterwards. Whether trout that are returned become uncatchable because they have learned to avoid the artificial fly is debatable.

As we move towards the millennium, more large fisheries may find it worth giving catch-and-release a try, or perhaps issuing a lower-priced ticket to anglers who don't want to kill trout. Toft Newton reservoir in Lincolnshire is already doing this.

Only in recent years have grayling gained recognition on some river fisheries. Old-fashioned river-keepers looked on them as vermin, saying they eat many trout eggs at spawning time. Too many grayling also meant too much competition for food for young trout, so heavy culling was practised. Now they are culled only when they prove a nuisance by over-breeding on certain stretches.

Catch-and-release grayling fishing has come to be practised more and more, and now rivers such as the Welsh Dee regularly produce specimens up to 2lb, while on some rivers where brown trout fishing has deteriorated, the grayling is filling a fly-fishing gap.

157

The fish has been hooked, played out and is being released by a happy fly-fisher. This is how it must be for the future as far as wild browns are concerned.

INDEX

158

160